THE HISTORY

COMMERCIAL ADVANTAGES

AND FUTURE PROSPECTS OF

BAY CITY

MICHIGAN.

LOCATION, POPULATION, RAILROAD AND SHIPPING FACILITIES,
MANUFACTURING AND COMMERCIAL ADVANTAGES,
MUNICIPAL GOVERNMENT, CHURCHES,
SCHOOLS, CLIMATE, SOIL, AND
VARIOUS IMPORTANT
INDUSTRIES.

ALL PERSONS WHO ARE SEEKING FOR A FLOURISHING COMMUNITY, WITH MODERN ADVANTAGES SHOULD READ AND CONSIDER THE CONTENTS OF THIS BOOK.

BAY CITY, MICH
PUBLISHED BY HENRY S. DOW
1875.

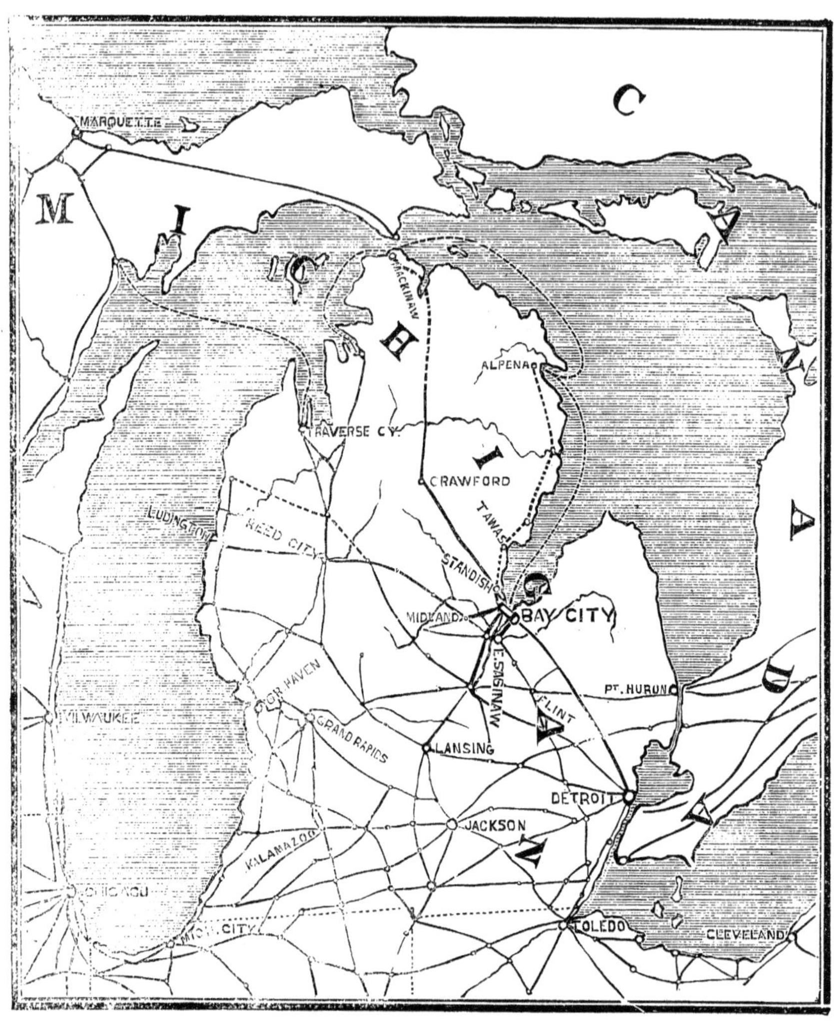

The above map shows the railroad connections at Bay City and the advantages for water and rail communication with all points East, West, North and South.

CONTENTS.

Important Figures.

We may be pardoned an apparent egotism as we point to the following brief comparative statement of the growth and progress of Bay City and its industries, satisfied that the showing will be acknowledged by all as creditable to the claim, that the time is not far distant when Bay City shall take rank as the second city of the State. Bay County was organized in 1857, although no county officers were elected until 1859; with this as a starting point, we present the following figures:

	1860.	1870.	1874.
Population	1,519	7,064	13,676
Assessed Valuation		$1,166,475	$1,782,250
Actual		$5,000,000	$9,000,000

Lumber manufacture, including only so much as is shown by Custom House books.

1865.	1868.	1873.	1874.
154,727,945	194,400,000	265.408,193	313,926,017

Salt, in Bay County, of which the majority is manufactured within the city limits, and the balance on the river banks contiguous to the city.

1865.	1873.	1874.
259,061 Bbls.	352,000 Bbls.	486,343 Bbls.

First National Bank Building.

First National Bank of Bay City.

The First National Bank of Bay City was chartered in May, 1864, with a capita of $50,000. In August, 1865, the capital was increased to $100,000.

About the first of February, 1868, the stock of the bank changed hands, and it may be considered that from that date the present institution has existed. The stock was increased to $200,000, and the following were the officers: James Shearer, President; B. E. Warren, Cashier, and N. B. Bradley, C. E. Jennison, A. S. Munger, A. Stevens, Directors.

The capital was further increased in January, 1872, to $250,000, and in July following it was made $300,000. The last increase was made in January, 1873, when the stock was made $400,000. This is the largest capital of any bank in the Saginaw Valley, and there are but two banks in the State with greater capital.

The office of the First National Bank was in Shearer block on the corner of Center and Water streets until January, 1873, when it was removed to its present elegant edifice (a representation of which appears herewith) on the corner of Center and Washington streets. The new building is of Ohio sand stone without, and is finished with black walnut within. The whole is heated by steam. The vault, Director's office, desks and all the appointments are of a superior order. The building cost $45,000. The officers are as follows:

President, James Shearer.

Vice-President, N. B. Bradley.

Cashier, B. E. Warren.

Directors, James Shearer, N. B. Bradley, Henry C. Moore, W. C. Yawkey, J. F. Eddy, C. E. Jennison, B. E. Warren.

BAY CITY IN 1837.

The dock and warehouse stood at the foot of Center Street. The buildings to the left are Saginaw Bay Company's office, Globe Hotel, Jas. G. Birney's residence next, and Judge Campbell's residence to the extreme left on what is now Third Street.

THE HISTORY,

Commercial Advantages and Future Prospects

OF BAY CITY, MICHIGAN.

TRADITIONARY HISTORY.

THE Saginaw Valley, in the lower portion of which is situated the beautiful and flourishing city of Bay City, derived its name from the Indian appellation "O-saug-e-nong" meaning "The Land of the Sauks." All that is known of this region in centuries gone by comes down to us by Indian traditions. Only a few of these traditions have been preserved but as these are not conflicting in important respects they are accepted as truthful by those early settlers in Michigan who were personally acquainted with the leading Chiefs. From Nau-qua-chic-a-ming, now the head chief of the Chippewa nation, a very kind-hearted and respectable old Indian, fully four score years of age, residing adjacent to the Saginaw river only a few miles above Bay City, we have gathered the tradition anew and herewith give it as received through an interpreter, Mr. Louis Tromble, who speaks the Chippewa as fluently as he does the English and French.

Three hundred and fifty years ago the Sauks were a warlike and powerful tribe of Indians who held undisputed sway throughout all the region of country now known as eastern Michigan. The Saginaw Valley was regarded as the most attractive portion of the lake region. Game of all kinds abounded. The Buffalo, Elk and Moose roamed throughout the forests while fish abounded in the rivers and lakes. It was an Indian's earthly paradise. The Sauks grew strong and were dreaded by their less warlike yet equally brave foes, the Chippewas, Ottawas and their allies. They frequently went northward towards the Straits of Mackinaw and fought the Chippewas and Ottawas. They also fought the tribes to the south of them and those on the east across the lake in Canada. In their expeditions against other tribes they suffered great loss but usually came off conquerors. Finally they went north to do terrible battle against the Chippewas in the vicinity of Traverse Bay. The loss to the Chippewas was very great but it served to rouse them to acts of the most gallant daring. The Sauks had offered the greatest indignity known in Indian warfare. They had captured and brought south as prisoners a Chippewa Indian and his squaw. This was defiance to the Chippewa tribe. But though conquered they were not vanquished nor subdued in spirit. Immediately after the Sauks started leisurely on their return to the Saginaw Valley the Chippewas with their allies organized a powerful force of not less than 3,000 warriors and in canoes came by way of the Straits of Mackinaw down the shore to near such point as they expected the Sauks would reach the Saginaw Bay. This was not far from the mouth of Pine river. The Chippewas reconoitered their position and followed them stealthily for several days until the Sauks had passed up the Saginaw river from its mouth to Skull Island, only a short distance above where John McGraw & Co.'s saw-mill now stands. The Chippewas halted at the mouth of Squaconning creek, near where Stevens & Shailer's mill is located. The head Chief was satisfied that Skull Island was to be made the scene of a great banquet or feast in honor of the victory the Sauks had achieved. This he therefore decided should be the time and place of a terrible conflict. First of all he desired to ascertain the exact location and surroundings of the Sauk's camping ground. To gain this information required the most trustworthy and daring spies. The Chief called for volunteers from his powerful young braves and of the number who came forward he selected three and sent them by night with instructions to penetrate to the very camp of the Sauks. How skilfully this service was performed the sequel shows. One of the scouts, while lying near the camp of the Sauks, spying out their position from the deep darkness surrounding, saw the Chippewa squaw approaching while on her way to bring water, she being required to do the service of a slave. The scout spoke to her in the language of his tribe and induced her to come so near that they could converse. He learned that on the following night there was to be a great feast and gave her such instructions as might save her life and that of her husband. The scout told her that at the approach of daylight, when the feasting and drinking had all ended and the camp was in a deep sleep, the Chippewas would suddenly and quietly enter and commence a dreadful massacre. To save the lives of the Chippewa and his squaw they were directed to lie on their faces and when kicked or struck to endure it all without raising their heads or in any way showing signs of life.

The situation having been ascertained, the scouts returned speedily and made their report. Preparations were at once made to execute the plan of the massacre, and accordingly when revelry was to reign in the camp of the Sauks the Chippewas landed on the south side of the island their main force, while the balance returned to the opposite side with their canoes, so as to prevent the escape of any Sauks by that route.

Who can fitly describe the occasion and the scene of that bloody massacre? Here was the flower of the forces of the dreaded Sauks returned from a great battle with victory and defiance perching on their plumes. They had gained victories before, but this last was the most important of them all. They felt themselves to be the undisputed owners of all the great lake region, and as a fitting demonstration their glory was to be crowned by a lordly feast. There were the revengeful and desperate Chippewas, writhing under the mortification of defeat and the defiance of their enemies in holding prisoners of their tribe as slaves. They were wary yet daring, knowing full well that if in this expedition they failed all would be lost, and they must retire from these favorite hunting grounds bequeathed by their fathers. They were ready to do and die in a struggle to regain honor and possession of what seemed their rightful dominion.

All the arrangements having been perfected, the stealthy foes of the Sauks, on the morning after the banquet, quietly invaded the camp wherein all were probably sleeping except the prisoners, and the massacre was soon commenced. The terrible work was speedily consummated, and the tradition is that not one of the Sauks escaped death.

The Chippewas remained in undisputed possession of the Saginaw

NAU-QUA-CHIC-A-MING,

Head Chief of the Chippewa Indians.

NAU-QUA-CHIC-A-MING, whose portrait above is from a photograph recently taken by Scotford, is probably nearly ninety years old, but as he does not know exactly, his age is uncertain. He was made one of the Chiefs of his tribe on the death of his father, since which time he was constituted head Chief. Nau-qua-chic-a-ming has been well and favorably known to all the early white settlers in the Saginaw Valley. His honesty and friendship have been proven in numberless instances. Since the above was put in type we learn that Nau-qua-chic-a-ming has gone to the "happy hunting ground." His death occurred on the 26th of October, 1874.

region until by the treaty of 1819 they ceded all but about 40,000 acres of the territory to the United States government, chiefly through the influence of Stephen V. R. Reilly, an Indian trader who married a squaw, and Jacob Smith, another trader. Reilly's children were regarded as Indians by the natives of the forest. The reservation was on the opposite side of the river, near Bay City. This reservation was sold to the government in 1837, according to terms of a treaty hereinafter set forth. Nau-qua-chic-a-ming, whose portrait we give herewith, accompanied the other chiefs of his tribe, and several white men to Washington for the purpose of perfecting the sale. The names of the chiefs are given as follows: Okemaw-ke-ke-to, Shaw-e-be-no-se, Wos-so, To-na-dog-a-ne, Mozhe-ga-shing. The white men were Henry Connor, Gardner D. Williams, Capt. J. F. Marsac, Charles H. Rodd, a half-breed, and Benj. O Williams.

When, in 1831, the French traveler and *savant,* De Tocqueville, visited America, he sought the wilds of what was then the "far west," and selected the lower portion of the Saginaw Valley from which to make observations. In his "Democracy in America," he wrote of this country with the pen of true prophecy when he said:

"In a few years these impenetrable forests will have fallen; the sons of civilization will break the silence of the Saginaw; the banks will be imprisoned by quays; its current, which now flows on unnoticed and tranquil, through a nameless waste, will be stemmed by the prows of vessels. We were perhaps the last travelers allowed to see the primitive grandeur of this solitude."

All that this illustrious writer could have anticipated, much though it may have been, is now a glorious reality; while what the future is yet more fully to develop, the careful reader of the follwing pages may reasonably judge from what has already been accomplished.

PIONEER HISTORY.

STEPHEN V. R. RILEY had three sons named respectively John, Peter and James. During his residence among the Chippewas he exercised a great influence over them—so great that it was found necessary on the part of the United States to conciliate him before a favorable treaty could be made with the Indians. That was done by allowing him to select six hundred and forty acres of land for each of his three sons, which was to be withheld from sale by the Indians, and the title to be confirmed by the United States, respectively to each of the above named half-breeds. The request came from the Indians that those reservations should be made, and the Government found it necessary to grant it. Mr. Riley, being a shrewd man, in his peregrinations among the Indians must have become acquainted with this region of the country, which knowledge would enable him to select the most valuable locations to be reserved for his sons. He located his eldest and favorite son (John) at the first eligible point for a town site after entering the river from the bay. It would seem that the region of country about the mouth of the Saginaw river was a favorite locality for the Indians, for the largest reservations they withheld from their sale to the United States were in that vicinity. Forty thousand acres were reserved on the west side of the river commencing at or near the mouth of Kawkawlin river, and extending back from the Saginaw at unequal distances far enough to make up the amount. On the east side of the Saginaw, commencing a short distance below the John Riley reserve, now included in the limits of Bay City, was the Naboabish reservation of two thousand acres, and there was another reservation of one thousand acres, a part of which is within the present limits of the Seventh ward of Bay City.

The first settler who resided any length of time within the present limits of Bay City was Leon Tromble, father of Mrs. P. J. Perrott

He was employed by the Government as an Indian farmer, and in the year 1831 he built a small log house on the John Riley reserve, which house was located between Water street and the river at a point about one hundred feet north of the *Chronicle* office. Mr. Tromble occupied that house till after the town of Lower Saginaw was laid out by the Saginaw Bay Company. In 1834 John B. Trudell, who married the eldest daughter of the late Benoit Tromble, built a log house at a point near the present residence of Mr. James Watson, where he resided till somewhere about 1850, when he removed to the west side of the river near where the Drake mill now stands. Afterwards in the year 1835, Joseph and Medor Tromble located the tract of land where the town of Portsmouth was afterwards laid out and built a trading house which they occupied, near the present site of the Center House, now in the Fifth Ward of Bay City. Benjamin Cushway, who was for many years employed by the Government as Indian blacksmith, about the same time built a dwelling house and shop on the west side of the river near the present residence of Mr. Frank Fitzhugh, in Salzburg. The parties above referred to made their location at this point on account of their connection with the Indian department and for the purpose of farming in a small way and trading with the Indians. They were the only settlers in this vicinity till 1836.

After General Jackson in 1833 caused the deposit of the surplus revenue of the United States to be withheld from the old United States Bank and deposited with the State Banks, large amounts accumulated in the vaults of the banks, which President Jackson encouraged the banks to loan to individuals by saying that it was by means of the trade of the merchants in paying the import duties on their merchandise into the treasury that the money had accumulated and it was no more than right that they should have the use of the money to facilitate the operations of their business. But by this hint to the banks they were not particular as to the business which the parties were engaged in who desired loans, and almost any one who was thought shrewd enough to make a good speculation by investing money could obtain loans from the banks. After the money was borrowed the point was to make a profitable investment of it, and nothing looked more attractive than the virgin soil of the West, where Uncle Sam possessed millions of broad acres which he would dispose of in parcels of forty acres or in other subdivisions of sections at the rate of one dollar and twenty-five cents per acre. Michigan was then, in 1836, considered the El Dorado of the West. A heavy emigration from New York and the New England States, having for three or four years previously directed its course to the beautiful Peninsula, so that at the time above mentioned, parties having money to invest thought it beyond doubt that if they should forestall those immigrants and purchase the land from the United States, they would receive a large advance on their purchases, from those who wished to make actual settlements. In view of the above-mentioned facts it was not likely that those speculators in casting their eyes over the map of Michigan, seeking a point within its borders for a place to make their investments, would overlook the Saginaw country, where the deep indentation of the Saginaw Bay penetrates the heart of the Peninsula and the branches of the broad river spread out in every direction like the branches of an enormous tree, the base of which is the medium through which the sap flows, as the outlet of the river is for the trade and commerce of a large portion of Northern Michigan.

Owing to the difficulty of access, Saginaw had but a small population at the commencement of the year 1836, but it had attained some notoriety. Saginaw City had been platted four or five years previously, and was supposed by many to be the only point on the river where a town was likely to be built. But others who were aware of the difficulties of ascending the river with heavy laden craft, and anticipating the vast commerce which the products of the Valley must eventually induce, conceived the idea of starting a town nearer the mouth of the river. With this view the Hon. Albert Miller purchased a tract of land from the Trombles and laid out the town of Portsmouth in July, 1836. At that time the whole of the west bank of the river from the mouth of the Kawkawlin to Willow Island (a point a short distance above W. R. Burt & Co.'s mill) was an Indian reservation. John Riley's reserve was the only other eligible point on the east side near its mouth for a town, and Riley had up to this time persistently refused to dispose of his land at any price. But during the summer of 1836 the pressure upon him to sell became so great that he was constrained to consult his father in reference to it. Stephen V. R. Riley was then and had for many years been the Postmaster of Schenectady, New York. His hair was as white as the snows of seventy or more winters could make it, but nothwithstanding his age he met John at Detroit and advised him to sell, and the title was soon after conveyed to Andrew T. McReynolds, then a prominent business man of Detroit, and F. H. Stevens, who was President of the Michigan State Bank, for a consideration of $30,000. The purchase was made for a number of prominent men of Michigan who afterwards formed a stock company and laid out the town of Lower Saginaw (now Bay City) on the tract of land above refered to. The Saginaw Bay Company consisted of Andrew T. McReynolds, F. H. Stevens, James Fraser, Henry R. Schoolcraft, Phineas Davis, Horace Hallock, John Hulbert and perhaps some others. After laying out the town they projected extensive improvements and commenced operations tending to the execution of their plans. A large hotel was framed and lumber provided for its completion ; a dock and warehouse were actually built, but in a few months a change came over the spirit of their dreams. The business of purchasing Government land with borrowed money had been carried on very extensively, and large sums of money in the form of State Bank currency had been turned over to the United States, when General Jackson with his usual shrewdness began to inquire as to the basis of the promise on the bills to pay their denominational value in specie. Upon investigation it was found that about all that the banks possessed with which to redeem their very large circulation was the Government deposits and the notes of the speculators who had purchased lands and gone into other visionary speculations. That called forth the specie circular which directed the custodians of the several land offices of the United States to receive nothing but specie in payment for lands. But that circular did not check at once the mania for purchasing Government lands. Bank bills could be procured and the banks were (in order to save their charters) compelled to pay specie for them on demand.

The Detroit Land Office, in which the lands in the northern portion of Michigan were subject to sale, was removed to Flint in the summer of 1836. There was then in that new town a small hotel near the banks of Flint river kept by "Bill Gifford," and during the autumn of that year there were nights when more than $40,000 in gold and silver was lying in different parts of the house, which had been brought by guests who were waiting for their turn to do business at the Land Office. But that state of things could not long continue. The specie was soon drawn out of the banks, a suspension of specie payments followed, and such a crash ensued as has never been known by the oldest inhabitant—one which will be remembered to the latest day of his life by every man who was then doing business. Upon that happening, the operations of the Saginaw

Bay Company were summarily suspended, and the towns of Lower Saginaw and Portsmouth, which so recently had been rife with business, and so promising of a prosperous future, dwindled to small hamlets surrounded by a howling wilderness with no prospect of improvement in the near future.

Many of the stockholders in the Saginaw Bay Company were in active business at the time of which mention has been made, and in consequence of the great disturbance in financial matters some were compelled to go into bankruptcy, while others suspended business operations and after 1838 no active operations were carried on by the Company as first organized. There is an instance on record where one of the original stockholders failed in business and had nothing better to turn over to one of his New York creditors than a narrow strip of land in Lower Saginaw, which was accepted because no better terms could be procured. Other losses consequent upon the times reduced the New York merchant so much that he found he had but little means except the strip of land in the wilds of Michigan, and after a few years he thought it advisable to come and see if there was any value in the land. He could not sell it but remained in charge of it till recently, when he passed away, having attained to the age of more than four-score years, leaving a fortune to his grandchildren of over two hundred thousand dollars, which was obtained solely on account of having accepted in payment of a debt what was then considered a piece of almost worthless land, from a bankrupt creditor.

After the great financial crash the Legislature of Michigan passed a general banking law, afterwards known as the "Wild Cat" system, which was intended to bridge over the "chasm," but it only plunged the people into a deeper one. There were two banks projected to be organized under the law above referred to, and located within the present limits of Bay City, to-wit: The Commercial Bank, of Portsmouth, to be located at Portsmouth, and the Saginaw County Bank, to be located at Lower Saginaw. A banking house was built for the Saginaw County Bank on the present site of Wallace's drug store in Bay City, and bills were engraved for each of the banks, but none were put in circulaiton except some of those of the Saginaw County Bank that were stolen while in transit from the engravers in New York, and the names of fictitious officers signed to them, which made them *just as good* as if they had been regularly issued under the law.

After every effort to keep the bubble inflated had failed the people became more interested in devising means by which they could obtain a livelihood than they were in building towns or making land speculations. Many, who a few months before were considered in affluent circumstances' found themselves without available means of support. The class that suffered least in the financial troubles were the farmers, which afterward induced many to turn their attention to that business, who had previously supposed they could get a living by their wits. After 1838 for several years the settlement and improvement of the country in the vicinity of the Saginaw river progressed slowly, and the growth of the towns on its banks was still slower. The Hon. Sidney S. Campbell, who removed to Lower Saginaw in the spring of 1838, was the first to make a permanent settlement here after the great financial crash. Although Lower Saginaw was at that time considered by many as a forlorn hope, it had many attractions for Judge Campbell, aside from his strong faith in its future greatness, in which he never wavered, and the fact that he could then obtain real estate here on very advantageous terms, he could gratify to his heart's content his passion for hunting. Besides other property, he purchased four lots where the Globe Hotel now stands (which he has been wise enough to hold on to), and from the frame of the kitchen part of the large hotel contemplated by the Saginaw Bay Company, he built what there was of the Globe Hotel till it was enlarged about ten years ago. It was the only public house in the place until 1851 or 1852.

But after the land came into market which the United States negotiated for by the treaty of 1837, (by the terms of which the Government was to cause the land to be surveyed and put into market at five dollars per acre, and held at that price for a certain length of time, and then what remained unsold should be reduced to a minimum of two dollars and a half per acre, and the Indians to receive the avails of the sales after deducting the costs of survey and sale and a large amount advanced to them with which to pay their debts) the attention of parties who had money was attracted to this part of the river. Doctor D. H. Fitzhugh purchased several parcels of land bordering on the river opposite Lower Saginaw and Portsmouth for five dollars per acre. This was about 1840. Previous to this Dr. Fitzhugh was a large landholder in the Saginaw Valley, but his purchases had been principally in the vicinity of Saginaw

City and points on the river above. Attracted by the superior advantages of a town situated near the mouth of the river, Dr. Fitzhugh, with the late James Fraser and the late Hon. James G. Birney, purchased the stock of the Saginaw Bay Company and became the proprietors of Lower Saginaw, and also of large tracts of land in the immediate vicinity of the town. Mr. Birney in 1842 removed with his family to Lower Saginaw. In 1844 he was a candidate for the Presidency of the United States, and the name of the place of his residence became more generally known. Mr. Birney, retaining his Southern ideas of the dignity of a farmer's life, and seeing the advantages this vicinity possessed for stock raising, in the early days of his residence here imported from the celebrated farm of Mr. Sullivant, of Ohio, some of the finest blooded Durham stock that was ever introduced into the State. That is one reason for the fine grade of stock that we see in this vicinity, which is descended from the native stock of early days, with which Mr. Birney generously allowed his Durhams to intermingle.

About the year 1846 there arose a demand for pine lumber, and it was thought by some that lumber could be manufactured from the excellent quality of pine (which could be had from the tributaries of the Saginaw for a little more than the cost of cutting and floating to the mills) that would pay a profit after deducting the cost of manufacturing and transportation to market. That year a man named Hopkins, and Mr. Pomeroy, (father of C. S. Pomeroy, of Bay City) in company with the late James Fraser, erected a steam saw-mill on the site which is now occupied by Gates & Fay's mill. The same year the Hon. Albert Miller and the late James J. McCormick repaired the old Portsmouth steam mill and cut a small amount of lumber. Some of the earliest shipments of lumber were made to Chicago. Vessels transporting grain from Chicago to Buffalo would, on their return trip, come into the river and load with lumber, but the lumber trade of Chicago was not large, as it then had to be carried into the country on wagons. But from the time above referred to the lumber business of the Saginaw Valley has been steadily increasing until it has assumed its present enormous proportions. The early manufacturers of lumber found but little profit in the business notwithstanding they had cheap pine and cheap labor. The projectors of the town had no idea of the vast amount of business that is derived from the salt and lumber interests but depended on other resources for business, some of which are shadowed forth in these pages.

Now when we take into consideration the wealth and business prosperity to which this city has attained, without drawing upon the elements which usually make up the business of a town (with which this city is abundantly supplied), we may consistantly anticipate for it a prosperous future.

The foregoing is a brief outline of the early history of a point which has been looked upon by some for the past forty years as the future mart for the products of Northern Michigan, but which did not really commence its growth till about the time of the commencement of the war of the rebellion. Its rapid growth since that time and its elements for future growth and prosperity may be ascertained in a measure by perusing what is hereinafter set forth in this work.

BAY CITY PIONEERS.

Many names of early settlers in this vicinity are here mentioned, some of whom have removed to other localities; some have "passed to the bourne from whence no traveler returns;" while a few yet remain who have been identified with the business interests of the place since its history commenced. Among those who have passed away may be mentioned the name of Albe Lull, who built a house in Portsmouth in the winter of 1836-37, and resided there till the fall of 1837, when he died of a malignant type of fever. Mr. Lull had been a prominent man in his native State, Vermont, where he ably represented his constituency in the Legislature, but after sustaining heavy losses by fire and otherwise, he came to Michigan to repair his shattered fortunes, but was cut short in his expectations as above stated.

The late Thomas Rogers settled in Portsmouth in 1837. He was employed as blacksmith for the company that built the steam saw-mill at that place. He also had charge of the postoffice, as deputy under the Hon. Albert Miller, who was appointed postmaster of Portsmouth in 1836 by Amos Kendall, then Postmaster-General. Mr. Rogers carried the mail once a week between Portsmouth and Saginaw, in a canoe in the summer, and on the ice in the winter for a time, till the labor and expense far exceeded the compensation which he received from postage on letters and newspapers, when the office was discontinued. Afterwards, when the population had increased so as to warrant the expense of carrying the mail, Mr. Rogers received the appointment of the first postmaster of Hampton. He kept his office in his dwelling house, which was located in the house where the Shearer block now stands in Bay City. Mr. Rogers remained a much respected citizen till August 1852, when he was stricken with cholera, and passed away much lamented by all who knew him. About the same time Mr. Rogers' brother-in-law, Mr. Monroe, died of the same disease. The families of the two still remain, and are identified with the business interests of Bay City.

The late Capt. John S. Willson in 1840 located on a small farm which he purchased from J. F. Marsac. In 1842 Capt. Willson was employed by a company in Saginaw City to freight goods from Detroit to that place. He sailed the little sloop *Mary*, the first regular trading vessel on the Saginaw River. In 1844, while on his way from Detroit with a cargo of provisions, etc., he was caught out in a gale and driven to the Canada shore, and for several weeks nothing was heard of him. During his absence his eldest daughter died. Capt. Willson took great pride in his orchard, which was about the earliest that was planted in this vicinity, and during his lifetime watched it with jealous care, not permitting it to be encroached upon by city improvements. But, since his decease, it has had to succumb to the destiny of all cherished objects that obstruct the growth of a thriving city. Capt. Wilson and his wife both passed away within a few years past, leaving a handsome property to be divided among their seven children.

Capt. Lyman Crowl was a resident here from 1849 to 1853. He was a partner in the firm of Russell, Miller & Co., which was for that time doing an extensive lumber business at Portsmouth. Capt. Crowl removed to Otisville, where he died in 1860. Jacob H. Little has since 1850 been identified with the business interests of Bay City, and is now the head of the grocery firm of Little & Delzell.

J. S. Barclay, who from a small beginning soon attained to prominence in the business interests of the place, built the Wolverton House, which,when completed, was the best building in the town. H. C. Scott. was an early settler and property holder in the place. He died at his residence near N. B. Bradley's mill some years since. His sons are in business near that point. Capt. George Rabey settled here as early as 1843. He resided in this vicinity till 1859, when he died at Portsmouth. Capt. Rabey was identified with the early marine of the river, having sailed the schooner North America in 1837 and 1838, which was then the largest vessel that had ever floated on the waters of the Saginaw river.

Capt. B. F. Pierce settled in what is now Bay City as early as 1839, and has since then been engaged in different branches of business. At one time he was a hotel-keeper, and also extensively engaged in the fishing business. He built the second warehouse that was erected on this part of the river, and was the owner of the first steam tug that ever towed a vessel on the Saginaw river. For a few years past he has not been so actively engaged in business, and is now living at Wenona, in easy circumstances and in comparative retirement from business.

Edwin Parks and Curtis Munger came here in the fall of 1848. They were first engaged in the cooperage business, and had the misfortune to have their shop burned with all their tools and clothing during the first winter in Bay City. But such trifles did not daunt them. They soon procured more tools, worked during the winter at their trade, commenced fishing in the spring, had a good season's business, and afterwards commenced in the mercantile business in a small way. In a few years they were joined by A. S. Munger, a brother of Curtis. Since then the operations of the Munger's need not be detailed for the information of any one acquainted in Bay City. A sight of their brick blocks, stores and improved farms will give a better insight to their business capacity and enterprise than can be portrayed with ink on paper.

Cromwell Barney was prominently identified with the early history of the place; he, with Albert Miller and B. K. Hall built the first steam saw-mill that was put in operation at this end of the river, and the second in the Saginaw Valley. Mr. Barney came to Portsmouth, which is now a part of Bay City, in the fall of 1836, when the whole region was a wilderness. He engaged in the enterprise of building a mill under such difficulties as would have discouraged any but the bravest heart and most determined will. After the mill was completed he disposed of his interest in it, and after building for Judge Campbell the old part of the Globe Hotel, he became a partner with the late James Fraser in building and running the Kawkawlin mill, till a short time previous to his death, which occurred in 1854.

In the fall of 1850 Alexander and William McEwen came to Bay City and commenced the erection of their mill at Woodside, which is now in the First ward of Bay City. In the spring of 1851 they were joined by their brother John. The mill was put in successful operation and run by the three brothers till the death of Alexander in 1853, since which time the business operations of William and John McEwen, collectively and individually, have served greatly to enhance the growth and prosperity of Bay City. They are both at the present time prominent business men of the city, and it is hoped by all good citizens that they may long remain so.

Charles E. Jennison came to this place in 1850 and commenced the mercantile business in company with the late James Fraser. After continuing in the partnership for about eighteen months he purchased Mr. Fraser's interest and continued the business alone till 1854, at which time he was joined by his brother, the late H. W. Jennison. After that the business was enlarged and carried on under the name of C. E. Jennison & Bro., till the death of the brother, which occurred in 1864. He was cut off in the vigor of his manhood and usefulness, and the people of Bay City felt that they had been called upon to part with one of the most useful and prominent members of society. Not long after the occurrence just referred to Charles E. Jennison sold out his mercantile business in order that he might give his whole attention to his greatly increasing general business. During the continuance of his successful mercantile business he was wise enough to invest all the surplus profits in real estate, which has made him one of the most successful business men in the Saginaw Valley, and perhaps the wealthiest in Bay City. Mr. Jennison's sterling business qualifications have served greatly to promote the interests of the city, and it is hoped they will long continue so to do.

In 1850 Mr. James Watson, who had been long known as a merchant of Detroit of the firm of J. & J. Watson, determined to seek a location for his business in some of the new prospective cities of the State. In seeking a point at which to locate his steps were directed to the Saginaw Valley. He came to Saginaw City where he met his old time friend, James Fraser, who, being desirous of securing an acquisition to the business interests of the Valley, descanted freely on all the advantages that town possessed, for at that time Saginaw City was the only town in the Valley where there was any show of business. After looking the ground over at that point, they came together to this part on the river. Mr. Watson's remarks were few but his foresight keen. After satisfying himself and selecting such pieces of property as he desired to purchase, he told Mr. Fraser he had determined to locate here if he could make such terms as he proposed. Mr. Fraser being agreeably surprised to hear such a determination expressed, readily acceded to Mr. Watson's terms and a bargain was soon consummated. With other property Mr. Watson purchased the dock and warehouse which was then standing at the foot of Center street. The warehouse was soon converted into a store and filled with one of the largest stocks of goods that had ever been brought into the Valley. This was late in the fall of 1850 and some of Mr. Watson's friends expressed surprise that he should have purchased so large a stock of goods for such an out of the way place, but before the breaking up of winter Mr. Watson had to send six teams to Detroit each to bring a load of goods to supply the demand. (It must be remembered that at this time in winter the only method of transporting merchandise to points north of Pontiac was by teams.) About this time was the first revival of business in this Valley, after the great depression in 1837 and 1838. A large amount of furs were brought to market, the fishing busi- was carried on quite extensively and the lumber business was just commencing. Mr. Watson was interested with Col. Henry Raymond in the lumber business—their mill being that now owned by James Shearer & Co., it having been built by Col. Raymond in 1850. Mr. Watson retired from the mill and carried on other branches of business, never forgetting to purchase real estate whenever an opportunity presented itself. By that means and through his indomitable energy and excellent business qualifications he has become one of the *heavy* men of the Saginaw Valley. Since Mr. Watson's first location at this point he has had the most implicit faith in its future growth and prosperity. In early years, when his neighbors would sometimes get discouraged with the slow progress the town was making, Mr. Watson would always cheer them with a picture of its future greatness which was ever in his imagination. And at the present time Mr. Watson's faith in the future prosperity of Bay City is as firm, and his energy to promote it as great as at any former period.

Col. Henry Raymond, who has been mentioned in this connection, has, since 1850, been prominent in the business interests of the town, having been frequently called upon by his fellow citizens to fill positions of responsibility and trust till recently, on account of failing health, he ha been compelled to seek a more genial clime on the shores of the Pacific.

J. B. and B. B. Hart came to Bay City in the fall of 1846. At that time there were but few white people in this vicinity. The

Messrs. Hart established a trade with what few whites were here, but a more extensive one with the Indians. In early years they were largely engaged in the fur and fish trade, and later either by themselves or in connection with others, in extensive mercantile operations. More recently Mr. B. B. Hart, with Dr. Geo. E. Smith, has been engaged in the manufacture of lumber and salt, and after disposing of that business the Messrs. Smith and Hart carried on a heavy grocery trade till about one year since they sold their business.

Dr. George E. Smith, referred to above, came to Bay City in 1850 and was for some time the only physician in the vicinity, but after others of his profession came to the town he retired from practice and gave his attention to other branches of business. He kept the first drug store in the town, was for some years postmaster and afterwards engaged in business with Mr. Hart as above mentioned and is now a much respected citizen without active business.

Israel Catlin was an early resident in this region having been engaged by Fraser and Barney as early as 1844 in building and superintending the running of the mill at Kawkawlin where he remained for a year or two. He came to this city and in company with the late James Fraser built the steam saw mill which is now owned by H. M. Bradley & Co., which he run successfully for a number of years. He sold out and afterwards formed a copartnership with Mr. Arnold, of Wenona, adjoining Bay City, where they carry on an extensive business in the manufacture of doors, sash and blinds. Mr. Catlin resides in Bay City, a much honored citizen. He was for several years postmaster and has for some years past occupied the responsible position of a superintendent of the poor for Bay County, and is now President of the Pioneer Society of Bay County. Elijah Stanton should be mentioned in this connection, he having erected as early as 1851 one of the mills owned by H. M. Bradley & Co. Mr. Stanton continued in the lumber business but two or three years when he sold and has since been extensively engaged in farming. He continues to reside in Bay City, and among other duties is engaged in assisting poor soldiers to procure their bounties and pensions from the Government.

Captain Joseph F. Marsac has long been known and identified with the interests of the Saginaw Valley, but for many years past more especially with Bay City. Capt. Marsac was an interpreter for the Government at the Cass treaty of 1819, which has been referred to. He was then a resident of Hamtramack, near Detroit, in which vicinity he resided till in 1838 he removed his family to Portsmouth, now Bay City, where in the succeeding year he purchased from the Government the tract of land upon which he resided till 1856. He sold to H. D. Braddock & Co. The tract is now in the Seventh Ward, and is known as the Ingraham property. After this sale Capt. Marsac removed to the adjoining tract on the south, where he still resides. During Capt. Marsac's long life, of over eighty years, he has had large experiences and passed through many vicissitudes. To recount them all would require a volume instead of a page. He was born near Detroit in 1793, and from that time has been a resident of Michigan, during which time the territory northwest of the Ohio river, (which had the name on maps of the Northwest Territory) has been transformed from a vast wilderness, (inhabited only by the red men with a few small settlements of whites near the principal water courses,) into ten populous States teeming with activity, wealth and refinement; within the borders of which cities have been built that rival in magnitude any that existed on this continent at the time referred to. Few persons have lived to see such great changes take place within the limits of the territory in which they were born. The increasing value of Capt. Marsac's early purchases of real estate has kept him in easy circumstances, and he is now enjoying his old age freed from the cares of business, and his hospitality and genial companionship greatly endear him to all his acquaintances.

The late James and James J. McCormick were early settlers of this city. James McCormick settled with his family at Flint in 1832, where he remained till the spring of 1834, when he removed with his family to a point on the river thirty miles below Flint, and settled on the old Indian fields, which he leased, it being contiguous to their village, Pe-wan-a-go-wink, where he lived in great harmony and friendship with his Indian neighbors, who, during his residence at that point, were almost the only neighbors he had. Mr. McCormick remained at Pe-wan-a-go-wink till 1841, when he removed to Portsmouth, at a point which is in the Fifth ward of Bay City. He soon afterwards purchased the building known as the Centre House, in the same ward, where he resided with his family till the spring of 1846, when he departed this life at peace with all the world. Mr. McCormick was "an honest man, the noblest work of God." He lived respected and died lamented by all who had ever known him. James J. McCormick, at the time of his father's removal to Bay City, had recently been married, and with his young wife accompanied his father to this point, which was their home during the remainder of life. On their arrival at Portsmouth the father and son fitted up the old steam mill at Portsmouth, which after the crash in 1837 had been some time idle. They together carried on the business of manufacturing lumber till the decease of the elder Mr. McCormick, after which Hon. Albert Miller became a partner in the mill with James J. McCormick, and they carried it on together till the spring of 1840, when in order that Mr. McCormick might gratify his desire for exploring the newly-discovered gold-fields of California, Judge Miller purchased his interest. Mr. McCormick accompanied one of the first caravans that crossed the plains in 1849. From earliest childhood he was trained to the habits of industry and economy. Having naturally a strong constitution, it was fitted for endurance. In his youth he was transferred to the wilds of Michigan, where many privations had to be endured. Later, in carrying on the lumber business, his inventive and mechanical genius had to be taxed to the uttermost. In taking charge of a dilapidated mill he became his own engineer, and lacking portions of machinery, both of wood and iron, these had to be supplied by the work of his own hands; so that the prospect of a four or five months' journey in the wilderness had no terrors for him, for his mechanical skill and strong arm had so well served him in every emergency. If there had been any lack of courage or of a determined will to persevere, Mr. McCormick's first experience would have deterred him from making the journey to California. He prepared his outfit and got ready to start with a wagon drawn by a yoke of oxen, just after the river broke up in the spring of 1849. At that time there was no ferry across the river at Bay City, and no passable road to Saginaw. All the communication by land was on the west side of the river across the prairie.

To overcome the difficulties in the way of starting on his journey, Mr. McCormick shoved a raft of flatted timber from Portsmouth against he current to the point above known as the Elbow, where he drove his eam on to the raft, ferried across the river and passed over the prairie o Saginaw, where he again had to cross the river. Perhaps Mr. McCormick had no experience on the whole journey that taxed his courage and energies more than that at the outset. He remained in California two years and a half, returning with something to compensate him for his hazardous undertaking and hard labor. After his return, he, with the Hon. S. S. Campbell, built a mill on the present site of Webster's mill, in the Fifth ward. Mr. McCormick afterwards purchased Judge Campbell's interest, and for some years carried on a very successful lumber business. He built a palatial residence, which he occupied till about two years ago, when he had to leave it forever and pass to realities of an unseen world. He leaves a widow, one son and one daughter and numerous relatives and friends to mourn his loss.

Dr. Daniel H. Fitzhugh, who has been mentioned in another connection as one of the early proprietors of Bay City, has never had a permanent residence here, but he has been familiar with all the interests of the Saginaw Valley since he first came here in 1835. During his frequent visits since that time he must have observed with great satisfaction, the growth and prosperity of the different towns on the river, for he is a property-holder in every part of the Valley. Especially of late, to see the many improvements made in Bay City contiguous to his large possessions, which serve greatly to enhance their value, must be very gratifying to him. Although Dr. Fitzhugh is an octogenarian he has the vigor, both mental and physical, of a man of forty, and from present appearances another decade may be added to his already long life.

Daniel H. Fitzhugh, Jr., came to Bay City in 1843 and built a large dwelling house (for that time) on the corner of Third and Water streets, which was afterwards occupied by his brother, William D. Fitzhugh, till it was destroyed by fire. D. H. Fitzhugh, jr., remained in Bay City at first but two or three years, when he went East and was engaged in the brokerage business in New York for some years. About five years since he returned to Bay City for a permanent residence. The northern extension of the J., L. & S. R. R. serves as a means by which Mr. Fitzhugh can gratify his early taste for hunting and fishing. Mr. Fitzhugh was the first to discover the habits and cause to be properly classified the fish known as the grayling, which are abundant in the waters of the northern portion of our peninsula. In after years those who have in any way been instrumental in promoting the interests of fish culture will be looked upon as benefactors of the human race.

William D. Fitzhugh was a resident of Bay City from about 1850 to

1856, when he was induced by his father-in-law, Hon. Charles Carroll, to return to Livingstone county, N. Y., for a permanent residence. During Mr. Fitzhugh's residence here he took an active part in promoting the growth of the town, was entrusted with the office of Supervisor of the township, and was otherwise honored by his fellow-citizens. After the house hereinbefore referred to was destroyed by fire, he built the residence on the corner of Tenth and Washington streets now owned and occupied by his brother, Charles C. Fitzhugh. Mr. Wm. D. Fitzhugh is a large property-holder in and about Bay City, and has recently been a great benefactor to the city by donating a fine tract of land for a park, which is now being improved for that purpose.

Charles C. Fitzhugh has been an honored citizen of Bay City and identified with its interests since about the time that William D. left the place. He attends to his own and his father's large real estate interests in this vicinity, which occupies his time except an occasional hunting tour for recreation in the northern woods.

The Hon. James Birney, eldest son of the late Hon. James G. Birney, who has been mentioned in another connection, may now be considered a pioneer in Bay City, having himself resided here since the summer of 1856, and his family since 1857. Mr. Birney purchased the interest of his co-heirs in his father's estate and made other large purchases of real estate in the vicinity of the city, that identified him at once with its interests, which he has endeavored to promote with the means he has had at command for that purpose. Mr. Birney has done much for Bay City, not only in material improvements but in his advocacy of measures that conduce to the promotion of its growth. Judge Birney has not only a local but a State and National reputation. He has been Circuit Judge of his Judicial District, has served his constituency in the higher branch of the State Legislature, has been Lieutenant-Governor of the State, and is now one of the United States Commissioners for the Centennial celebration. Mr. Birney is now in the vigor of manhood and in all probability will long continue to exert an influence favorable to the growth of our thriving city.

The late James Fraser, who was an early settler of the Saginaw Valley, and of whom an interesting volume might be written, was virtually the father of Bay City. It was at his instigation that the purchase of the tract was made from John Reilly. He was a large stockholder in and principal manager of the Saginaw Bay Company, and after the disastrous financial crash of 1837, which affected Mr. Fraser less than any other man in Michigan who was doing the same amount of business, he and Dr. Fitzhugh and Mr. Birney purchased the whole stock of the company as has been mentioned before. The reason that Mr. Fraser was not involved in the disasters that overwhelmed all other dealers in real estate at that time, was the fact that he was during all the year 1836 selling lands at an enormous advance over their cost. Many of the stockholders of the Saginaw Bay Company became bankrupt, and a large share of the stock of the company was purchased at a nominal price, and the parties, having no financial embarrassments, were enabled to manage the property as they pleased.

The property was not held long in common by the three parties, a division being made and each party managing his own possessions. During the later years of Mr. Fraser's life, which terminated in 1865, he did much to promote the growth of Bay City, and erected the walls of the large and elegant hotel which bears his name, but was not permitted to see it finished and occupied.

Hon. Albert Miller came from Vermont in 1832 and has been in this region ever since. At first he lived in Saginaw City, then upon a farm on the Tittabawassee river, and finally in 1848, he removed to Portsmouth, now part of Bay City. He surveyed the town site of Portsmouth in 1836, and has ever since been very prominent in developing not only that locality but all the interests of the Valley. He was one of the builders of the second saw-mill on the Saginaw river.

Judge Miller has held many public offices of honor and trust. In 1835 Gov. Mason made him Justice of the Peace and Judge of Probate of Saginaw county, and he held the latter office by election for eight years thereafter. He was a member of the State Legislature in 1847,and has filled numerous township and city offices. He is an elder in the Presbyterian Church of Bay City, and President of the Saginaw Valley and Bay County Pioneer Societies. He has contributed, perhaps, more extensively than any other person, to the early histories of the Valley, manifesting in that, as well as in present industries and improvements, an intelligent interest and activity, which have made him a valuable citizen.

Bay County Court House.

COUNTY ORGANIZATION.

Bay County includes territory on both sides of the Saginaw river near its mouth. Its extreme length is eight townships, running from T. 13 N. to T. 20 N.; and its greatest breadth is five townships, running from Range 3 E. to Range 7 E. Out of this parallelogram, however, Saginaw bay takes a very large piece, and there are but fourteen organized townships in the county, not including Bay City. Almost the entire eastern boundary of the county is formed by the bay shore, which makes almost a semi-circle of it.

The county was organized in 1857. It is now a part of the Eighth Congressional District of the State; forms with Tuscola county on the east the Twenty-fourth State Senatorial District; and it forms the Eighteenth Judicial District, and a separate State Representative District.

The following table shows the several incumbents of county offices from the time of the organization of the county to the present year:

OFFICES.	1857.	1858.	1860.	1862.
Clerk, - - - -	Elijah S. Catlin	Thos. W. Lyon	S. W. Saylor	N. Whittemore
Prosecuting Att'y - -	C. H. Freeman	James Birney	T. C. Grier	L. Beckwith
Register of Deeds, -	T. M. Bligh	T. M. Bligh	F. A. Martin	Aug. Kaiser
Sheriff, - - - -	Nathan Simons	N. Whittemore	J. S. Barclay	R. H. Weidman
Treasurer, - - -	James Watson	James Watson	James Watson	A. S. Munger
Judge of Probate, - -	S. S. Campbell	S. S. Campbell	S. S. Campbell	S. S. Campbell
Circuit Court Com'r, -	S. P. Wright	W. L. Sherman	T. C. Grier	A. McDonell
Surveyor, - - -	J. J. McCormick	T. W. Watkins	B. F. Partridge	B. W. Seeley

OFFICERS.	1864.	1866.	1868.	1870.	1872.
Clerk - -	N. Whittemore	H. H. Wheeler	H. A. Braddock	H. A. Braddock	H. A. Braddock
Pros. Atty -	L. Beckwith	Isaac Marston	Isaac Marston	C. H. Denison	T. F. Shepard
Reg. of Deeds	B. Witthauer	B. Witthauer	T. A. Delzell	T. A. Delzell	H. M. Hemstreet
Sheriff - -	P. J. Perrott	J. G. Sweeny	P. J. Perrott,	Miron Bunnell	Miron Bunnell
Treasurer -	A. S. Munger	A. S. Munger	C. Munger	C. Munger	Chas. Supe
Judge of Probate	S. S. Campbell	S. S. Campbell	H. H. Hatch	H. H. Hatch	J. W. McMath
Cir. Court Com'r	A. McDonell	Wm. Daglish	H. H. Norrington	H. H. Norrington	J. L. Stoddard
Surveyor - -	J. M. Johnson	E. L. Dunbar	E. L. Dunbar	E. L. Dunbar	E. L. Dunbar

MUNICIPAL ORGANIZATION.

The village of Bay City was incorporated in 1859, and retained its village organization until 1865. The following table shows the principal village officers for the several years:

OFFICES.	1859.	1861.	1862.	1863.	1864.	1865.
President, -	C. Munger	W. L. Fay	Jas. Watson	C. Munger	C. Munger	J. B. Hart
Recorder, -	C. Atwood	S. S. Campbell	J. L. Monroe	N. Whittemore	N. Whittemore	P. S. Heisordt
Treasurer, -	J. F. Cottrell	B. Witthauer	Aug. Kaiser	C. Scheurman	C. Scheurman	E. Frank.

The village was made a city and elected its first Common Council in 1865. By the charter, the city government is vested in a Mayor and Council, the latter body having power to entrust certain duties to other bodies which it elects; and to certain specified officers which it also chooses. Thus, the management of the Water Works is entrusted to the Board elsewhere given, the Council passing upon all contracts and exercising a general supervisory power over its acts. In like manner, the Board of Education has immediate charge of the Schools, but though the Council elects the Board, the latter is independent of the former in all its acts, even to determining the amount to be raised by taxation for school purposes. The Council controls absolutely all other appointments and expenditures.

The officers elected by the Council are a City Attorney, a Marshal and such assistants as may be needed, a Director of the Poor, a Harbor Master, a Street Commissioner, and a certain number of Scavengers, with a Pound Master. The Fire Department organization, outside of the hose companies, consists only of a Chief Engineer.

The following table shows the several city officers since the first organization under the city charter:

OFFICES.	1865.	1866.	1867.	1868.	1869.
Mayor, - -	N. B. Bradley	Jas. Watson	Jas. Watson	W. L. Fay	J. J. McCormick
Recorder, -	W. T. Kennedy	W. T. Kennedy	N. Whittemore	N. Whittemore	N. Whittemore
Treasurer, -	E. Frank	E. Frank	E. Frank	E. Frank.	I. G. Worden
Controller, -	....	....	....	....	R. McKinney
OFFICES.	**1870.**	**1871.**	**1872.**	**1873.**	**1874.**
Mayor, -	A. S. Munger	G. H. Van Etten	G. H. Van Etten	G. H. Van Etten	A. Stevens
Recorder, -	N. Whittemore	I. G. Worden	I. G. Worden	I. G. Worden	I. G. Worden
Treasurer, -	Aug. Kaiser	L. S. Coman	L. S. Coman	L. S. Coman	L. S. Coman*
Controller, -	Geo. Lord	Geo. Lord	Geo. Lord	Geo. Lord	Geo. Lord.

*Resigned, and C. S. Braddock appointed by the Council to fill the vacancy.

POPULATION.

The federal census of 1870 gives Bay City a population of 7,064, and Bay county a total of 15,900. The State census taken in the Spring of 1874, or about three years after the last federal census, shows the city to have a population of 13,676—an increase of 6,612 in the time named, or very nearly doubling the inhabitants. The county had by the State census of 1874 a population of 24,801, an increase of 8,901 since 1870, or about 60 per cent. These figures are sufficiently suggestive of the surprisingly rapid development of both city and county. At the same rate of increase the city would number over 30,000 people at the next federal census.

The population of the city contains a large number of thrifty Germans, many industrious Canadian French, with Irish, Polanders, etc., in smaller numbers—all together a hardy and thrifty population, not given to turbulence. The prosperous condition of educational interests and churches shows the character of the people to be generally excellent.

Bay County Jail.

INDEBTEDNESS AND TAXATION.

The bonded indebtedness of Bay City, as shown by the Comptroller's report for 1874, is $312,320, divided as follows:

School	$ 49,570
City contingent fund	35,750
Water Works	227,000

Of the $227,000 water works bonds reported, only $206,000 had been negotiated at the date of the report, but the balance was needed to complete the work then ordered, and has since been negotiated. There is no floating indebtedness.

From the Comptroller's report we also learn that the Contingent Fund account—which includes generally all expenses except for schools, water works and special improvements—stood as follows for the preceding year: Receipts, $61,114.33; disbursements, $59,195.73—showing a balance of $1,918.60 on hand.

From the Treasurer's report to the Council for 1874, we take the following figures: The total receipts of his office for the year preceding were $209,803.03 ; and the total disbursements were $197,532.52—leaving a balance of cash on hand of $12,370.51.

For the indebtedness above exhibited the city can show its water works, its school property, and its fire apparatus—an amount in value largely in excess of the indebtedness. The school property, for instance, is constantly and rapidly increasing in value, speaking of it as if it were to be put upon the market for sale. The value of the water works increases, of course, as the system is perfected and brought into more general use throughout the city.

Valuations for taxation are supposed to be made upon the basis of one-fourth of the real market value of the property. The actual fact, however, is that the tax valuation is often but one-sixth of the true valuation. The assessment rolls for 1874 show the following as the total valuation :

Real estate.	$1,479,750
Personal	302,500
A total of	$1,782,250

This represents a valuation of $7,129,000 according to the supposed basis of one-fourth, and an actual valuation of nearly $9,000,000.

The amount of tax for city, highway and school purposes, and to pay interest on the bonded indebtedness, was as follows for 1874 :

City	$ 35,645
School	45,039
Bonded interest	26,256
Highway	7,293
A total of	$114,233

This is about 6 per cent. on the returned valuation, and not over one and one-fifth per cent. on the true valuation. The State and county levies are very small, and do not add materially to the tax-payer's burdens.

The city has no railroad bonds to provide for ; no ditching or dredging expenses to meet, thanks to her high and dry site on the river below all sand bars ; and no outstanding liabilities of any kind to provide for, except as above detailed. For this reason, the rate of taxation, as will be seen, compares most favorably with that of other Michigan cities, as to amount, while a comparison of objects of taxation will be still more in favor of Bay City. Whereas some neighboring places must annually expend considerable sums in ditching lands, filling up low places, or dredging the river channel to keep navigation unobstructed, Bay City has to tax her people only for such permanent and desirable improvements as they desire, and need sink no money in the bottom of the river or in the quagmires of bayous.

WATER WORKS.

In 1872 the city inaugurated a system of water works, designed first to afford efficient fire protection, and second to supply private consumers for domestic and other uses. The sum of $327,000 in bonds of the city, running for a term of years, has been voted by the people to complete the works. The works are under the immediate control of a Board of Water Commissioners chosen by the Council, as follows:

A. Walton, Thos. Cranage, Jr., Wm. Westover, Wm. Smalley, H. M. Bradley, Andrew Miller, Thos. H. McGraw.

Hon. Wm. Westover is President of the Board, and E. L. Dunbar is its Secretary and the Engineer of the works.

The engine house and pumping machinery are located in the northern part of the city. The machinery consists of duplicate sets of piston and rotary pumps, and is capable of pumping 3,000,000 gallons of water per day. It is reported to be, everything considered, the best machinery ever made by the Holly Company, and cost $32,000. The engine house, walls, foundations, etc., cost $22,000.

Ten miles of service pipe have been laid and are now in operation. The plan of this is such as to afford thorough fire protection to all the thickly settled parts of the city—to all, in fact, but the extreme outskirts. There were in August, 1874, private consumers of water to the number of 275, and the number was increasing steadily. Part of the manufacturing establishments avail themselves of the water works, the service being found very convenient in supplying steam boilers, washing out boilers and salt pans, etc.

The original plan contemplated a supply of water from Saginaw Bay, which would require to be brought about four miles from the bay to the pumping machinery. The cost of a large inlet pipe for this purpose will be about $90,000, and this has been provided for in the appropriations already made. The work is to be completed early in 1875, being now well under way. This will give an unlimited supply of absolutely pure water from the broad bay, a source which can never be contaminated. There is no other feature of the location of Bay City more valuable than this, which will give an abundant supply of the purest water for all purposes. The liberal outlay for this object will assuredly be returned a hundred fold in the improved health of a city so supplied.

The practical operation of the works here is in charge of Mr. A. B. Verity, long familiar with the Holly machinery, and a skilled engineer. He has also had more or less supervision of water works erected in this section, and his success, with the uniformly excellent results of the working of the Bay City machinery, attest his skill.

FIRE DEPARTMENT.

The fire department of the city formerly consisted of two steam fire engines, with hose carts, all drawn by horses. This apparatus is still retained by the city, but its use in the corporate limits has been effectually superseded by the introduction of the Holly water works and a fire organization especially adapted to serve them. The present fire department is upon the volunteer plan, and embraces five regularly organized hose companies, under a chief engineer. There are three horse hose carts in the department, and two which are drawn by hand. The companies are well supplied with hose, and their houses are located so as to give the best protection to all parts of the city, namely: One each in the First, Second, Fourth, Fifth and Seventh Wards. During the last year the department, using the Holly water, has several times checked conflagrations which would have effectually baffled the old organization and system, and has in this way paid for itself over and over. It may be set down as impossible for an extensive conflagration to occur within reach of the Holly water, and it is rare indeed that even a single frame building, though old and dry, is consumed. The efficiency of her fire protection is an object of just pride with Bay City.

POLICE REGULATION.

The regular police force of the city is an efficient patrol under a Marshal and an Assistant Marshal, both elected by the Council. The force is under strict rules and surveillance, and the public peace and quiet are well preserved. There are comparatively few liquor saloons in the corporative limits, and disreputable houses are scarcely known. All drinking places are required to be closed on Sunday, and the requirement is enforced. Though the city is frequently the temporary abiding place of hundreds of men on their way to and from the lumbering woods, the streets are always orderly.

STREET IMPROVEMENTS.

In street improvements Bay City is far in advance of any other Michigan city outside of Detroit. She has five streets paved with wood as follows:

Water street, from Third to Sixth, a distance of four blocks, or about 1,500 feet. This is the squared pine block pavement.

Center street, from Water to Johnson, a distance of seventeen blocks, or over 4,500 feet. This is partly the Nicholson, or squared pine block pavement, and partly the McGonegal, or irregular pine block.

Third street, from Water to Johnson, a distance of seventeen blocks, or about 4,500 feet. This is the Wyckoff wooden pavement, of cedar blocks, laid with top-dressing of tar and gravel.

Saginaw street, from First to Sixth, a distance of six blocks, or over 2,000 feet. This is the Wyckoff cedar block pavement.

Fifth street, from Water to Jefferson, a distance of four blocks, or something over 1,000 feet. This is also the Wyckoff cedar block pavement.

The city owns the Wyckoff patent on all its streets, and the cedar blocks are found to be the most durable and to make in every way the pleasantest pavement for travel.

Water street below Third and above Sixth, is planked, but will doubtless be paved in the course of another year. Washington street is also planked, but this will be replaced by pavement soon, as it would have been in 1874 had not so much work been ordered before the subject was agitated among the property owners on the street. Twelfth street is planked from Water to the Tuscola plank road, a distance of over a mile, and what is known as the Bullock road, in the Seventh ward, is planked out to the same road.

The city has many miles of graded streets, and nearly every street, even in the outskirts, is supplied with good plank sidewalks.

BANKS AND BANKING.

Bay City has four regular general banks, as follows:

First National, with a capital of $400,000. James Shearer, President; B. E. Warren, Cashier.

Second National, with a capital of $100,000. William Westover, President; W. L. Plum, Cashier.

State Bank, with a capital of $160,000. A. Chesbrough, President; Orrin Bump, Cashier.

Bay City Bank, capital $100,000. George Lewis, President; Geo. H. Young, Cashier.

In connection with the latter bank is a savings institution, having the same officers as the bank.

The Collection Bank of Bay City is a lately-established institution, of which G. A. Cooke is Cashier. Its business is indicated by its name, and its need is proved by its success.

The above list shows an aggregate banking capital of $760,000—an amount far below the needs of the vast business we have exhibited elsewhere in this work as belonging to this city. The entire Valley is deficient in banking capital, and in no instance is the amount so disproportioned to the business done as in this city.

COURTS.

The Circuit Court for Bay county holds three terms each year, beginning on the first Tuesdays of January, April and September. Hon. S. M. Green is Judge.

The Recorder's Court of Bay City is in session every morning at 9 o'clock, in the Council Chamber, Watson block. Hon. Isaac G. Worden, Recorder.

The Justices' Courts are located as follows: Justice John Hargadon, Justice Lawrence McHugh and Justice Nathaniel Whittemore, in Watson block. Justice Henry Miller, Water street, Seventh ward.

Hon. Luther Beckwith is United States Commissioner. Office in the Bank block, Center street.

Circuit Court Commissioner John L. Stoddard has his office in the Watson block.

The newly-elected Circuit Court Commissioners are Daniel Mangan and Hiram L. Blaisdell, and they take their offices in January, 1875.

CUSTOM HOUSE.

The custom house for the port of Bay City is located in the Maxwell block, Water street, convenient to the river and the steamer landings. Col. John McDermott is deputy collector. The port is in the District of Huron, and the jurisdiction of this office extends by custom and consent up the river as far as Zilwaukie, and to the various bay shore ports as far as Tawas in the north, and Port Austin to the eastward. Above Zilwaukee the business is taken care of by the East Saginaw deputy collector. At Tawas and Port Austin deputies have recently been appointed, greatly to the convenience of navigators.

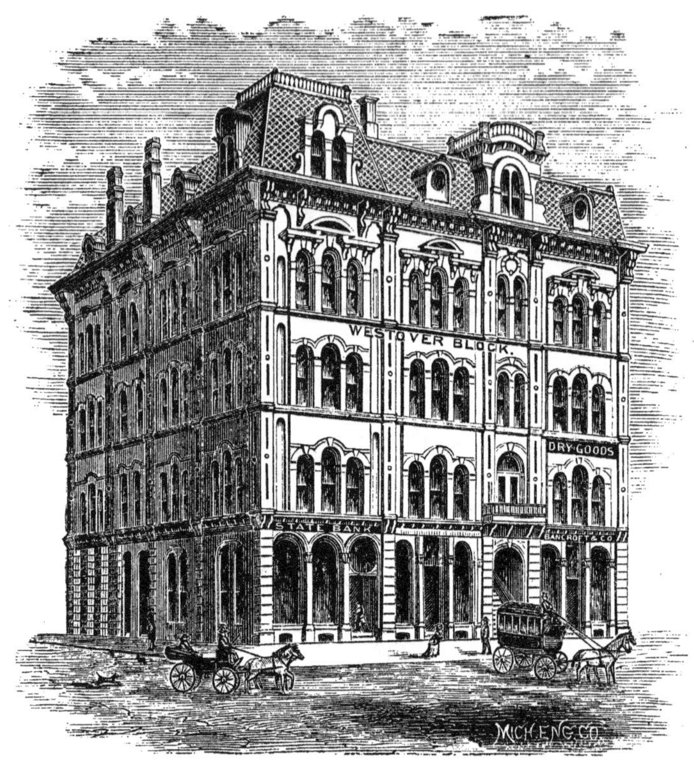

Westover Block.

PUBLIC BUILDINGS, BUSINESS BLOCKS, ETC.

In another part of this work will be found some descriptions of the school and church buildings of Bay City. Several of them are among the most sightly and beautiful of the public buildings of the city.

Among the notable structures of the town we name first the county buildings, standing on opposite sides of Center street, at a short distance from Water street, or very near the business centre of the city. The court-house is a very substantial and good-looking building, of brick, with a handsome lawn in front, ornamented with shrubbery and a large fountain. The court-room is said to be the best in the State, and is large and with high ceiling. The building is supplied with water throughout, and cost about $40,000.

Almost directly opposite the court-house is the county jail, a two-story brick building, very effectively ornamented, and making of what is usually only a unsightly pile of brick and stone, a noteworthy addition to the architectural adornments of the beautiful squares on which it fronts. The cost of the jail was about $35,000.

The Westover block (Opera House) is a four-story brick building, fronting on Center street, and in the heart of the city. The Opera hall is capable of seating comfortably 1,200 persons, and is one of the handsomest and best arranged places of amusement in the State.

The Cranage block was erected in 1873-4. It fronts on Center street and is one block above the Opera House. It is a three-story brick, with all the modern improvements, water and closets to the third floor, etc. The block has a front of 100 feet, and the first floor affords some of the finest salesrooms to be found in the city.

The Bank block is next west of the Cranage. At the end of this is the First National bank, in a building of three stories, with solid stone fronts on two streets, and very substantial and handsome.

Further down Center street is the Munger block, a three-story brick, elegantly fitted throughout, having handsome stores on the first floor, plate glass fronts, etc.

The Fraser House is a four-story and basement brick building, of good external appearance, and massive in its frontage on two streets.

Opposite the Fraser are the Shearer and Averell blocks, both three story brick, the former being on the corner of Water and Center streets, and containing four stores.

The Union block is on Water street opposite the Fraser House. It is a fine three-story brick building.

Next north of the last-mentioned building is the Watson block, a massive four-story brick, with French roof towering high, and making a sightly pile as one looks down Centre street.

Nearly opposite on Water street is the McCormick block, four stories in height, of brick, and having one of the handsomest fronts in the city.

Further down Water street, one block, is the McEwen block, 100 feet front, a three-story brick, of handsome appearance throughout.

Nearly opposite is the Jennison block, about 100 feet front, of brick, and as substantially and solidly built as any structure of the kind in the State.

Still further down Water street is the Birney block, a three-story and basement brick, of good external appearance.

On the corner of Third and Water streets, the Campbell House, a three story brick block, stands, and on the opposite corner is the Park block, also a three-story brick.

There are many handsome stores in blocks not enumerated above, some of the finest rooms for business being in single buildings of two stories, but the above are the principal of the large blocks. The whole business portion of the city is in remarkably good style, and the streets have a thrifty, clean look, which tells of rapid development.

PUBLIC LIBRARY.

The Bay City Library Association had a library of about 5,000 volumes, and in the spring of 1874 an arrangement was perfected for a union of this library with the public library, all to be under the care of the Board of Education. There was a balance of several thousand dollars to the credit of the public library fund, and a part of the agreement was to the effect that this balance should be expended as far as might be judicious in the purchase of new books. The fund was sufficient to ensure a large collection of books, and the library of the Association afforded a most excellent nucleus.

Fraser House.

HOTELS.

Bay City is comfortably provided with hotels, both as to number and quality. The Fraser House, a four-story brick, heads the list as the leading first-class house of the city. Its apartments are commodious and handsomely furnished, and its fare is of the best. The Campbell House comes next, a convenient three-story brick building, with a good number of well-appointed rooms, and everything in good style. There are many other good hotels of a less expensive sort, among which may be mentioned the Taylor and Astor houses in the southern part of the city, and the Globe, Wolverton, Forest City and others in the central part.

FISHERIES.

The fisheries on the river and the bay are by no means an unimportant interest. The catch comprises white-fish, and several less valued varieties of what are known as "soft" fish; muscalonge, pickerel, bass, lake trout, herring, and numerous other varieties most valuable for packing and transportation. The white-fish, pickerel, trout, etc., are especially fine. The catch is made with nets in the spring and fall, and in the winter hundreds of men make a good living by spearing pickerel through the ice on the bay. Large quantities of the fish are packed in ice in this city and shipped to various interior cities, while peddlers supply the country round about from wagons. The common price during an ordinary winter season is from six to nine cents per pound for pickerel on the ice where caught, while suckers and the like are "lumped off" at a cent apiece.

In 1870, according to statistics prepared by authority of the Legislature, there was $124,000 invested in fisheries in Bay, Alpena, Alcona Cheboygan and Iosco counties; the yearly catch was 16,330 bbls., valued at $156,350. Since that time the catch has largely increased, and for 1873 the operations of the fishermen on the bay and at the mouth of the river were estimated at 2,500 barrells, and of all the shore fisheries at 20,000 barrels.

PUBLIC PARKS.

Bay City is liberally supplied with public parks and pleasure grounds. The most central of these are the four squares on Center street, in the very heart of the city, upon two of which the county buildings front. The city has just erected two ornamental fountains upon the eastern squares, which are supplied from the Holly water works. In the yard of the county court house there is a larger fountain, and all these grounds are set with shade trees and shrubbery.

At a distance of about one mile from the river, and just to the north of Center street, is Carroll park, a tract of land given to the city by Mr. C. C. Fitzhugh for a park. The ground is partly wooded and partly open, and the city has already begun the improvement of it by the construction of well-turnpiked drives through the wooded portion in various directions. The tract is quite extensive, and will in time be a very convenient and attractive resort.

There are two other public parks in the city—one embracing the ground between Washington, Second, First and Jefferson streets, and one of the same size between Ninth and Tenth streets. These grounds have been set with ornamental trees, and will in time be very ornamental to their neighborhoods. The probability is that the extreme southern wards will soon secure the dedication of a suitable tract for a park in that locality.

It will be seen that in all the haste and bustle of a rapidly growing and always busy city, matters of beauty and healthfulness have received due attention.

CEMETERIES.

Pine Ridge Cemetery was laid out by Hon. James Birney. It is well located on the Tuscola plank road, near the city limits, and the grounds are sufficiently extensive and have been considerably improved. There are several private vaults and monuments of more than ordinary excellence in design and execution.

The Catholic Cemetery is located south of Pine Ridge, and has ample grounds, well kept.

Cranage Block.

CIVIC SOCIETIES.

We give below a list of the various Masonic and other societies of Bay City. This list includes all the most prominent organizations, though there are several of less importance which are not noted :

MASONIC.

The hall of the Masonic Societies is in the McCormick block, Water streets. The societies are :

Bay City Commandery, No. 26, K. T.

Blanchard Chapter No. 59, R. A. M.

Joppa Lodge, No. 315, F. A. M.

Bay City Lodge, No. 129, F. A. M.

Portsmouth Lodge, No. 190, F. A. M.

There is also a lodge of colored Masons.

I. O. O. F.

The following are the organizations:

Bay City Lodge No. 204.

Humboldt Lodge No. 154.

Kenonda Encampment.

Grace Lodge No. 19, D. R.

Valley Lodge No. 109.

I. O. G. T.

Bay Lodge No. 104.

Portsmouth Lodge No. 109.

I. O. B. B.

Independent Order of B'nai B'rith.

MILITARY.

Peninsular Military Company, of Bay City. (Co. E., Second Reg't Mich. Infantry).

MISCELLANEOUS.

Bay City Typographical Union, No. 153.

Bay County Bar Association.

St. Andrew's Society.

St. Patrick's Society.

Bay County Medical Society.

Regular Bay County Medical Society.

Homeopathic Society.

Lafayette Temperance Society.

German Workingmen's Society.

St. James R. C. Total Abstinence Society.

St. Joseph's R. C. Benevolent Society.

Teutonia Society.

Bay County Agricultural Society.

Bay City Turners' Society.

Bay County Board of Fire Underwriters.

I. K. U. K. Club, (a social club of Bay City).

Bay City Boat Club.

St. Stanislaus Kotska Society (Polish).

First Baptist Church of Bay City.

CHURCHES.

The above cut represents the house of worship of the First Baptist church, in Bay City. It takes rank with the best specimens of church architecture in the west, being excelled by few, if any, in this State. It is built of brick, in the style of the decorated Gothic of the Fourteenth Century. The door-caps, window-caps, water-tables and buttress offsets are of cut stone. The roof is slated in green and black, fancifully patterned, and is surmounted with handsome crestings. Its two spires rising, one to the height of 130 feet, the other 180 feet, are visible not only from all parts of the city, but attract the eye from a range of three or four miles beyond the city limits.

The extreme length of the building is 140 feet, and its greatest width 72 feet. The audience room is 54x94 feet, finished in black walnut and ash, the seats made comfortable with hair cushions, covered with crimson rep, and the floor covered with a Kidderminster carpet, made to order at that celebrated factory in England. The windows are of stained glass, arranged in highly ornamental designs. The ceiling is frescoed in soft tints. An organ of nearly 1,400 pipes, above and in the rear of the pulpit, adds greatly to the general good effect, both upon the eye and the ear of the worshipper. In the rear of the audience room are church parlors, kitchen, robing rooms, lecture and Sunday-school rooms. From the steam heater in the basement, to the bell of over 3,000 pounds weight in the belfry, the greatest convenience and completeness seem to be very nearly attained. The edifice is an ornament and a credit to the city, as it represents the enterprise, taste and liberality of the community at large, as well as of the Society to which it belongs.

The First Baptist church and society was organized July 10, 1863. On the 10th day of the following month they entered their newly-completed house on Washington street, which was almost entirely a gift from the late James Fraser. The first pastor was the Rev. Franklin Johnson, now pastor of the First Chuch, in Cambridge, Mass. Following him was the Rev. S. L. Holman, whose brief pastorate was succeeded by the ministry of the lamented Patterson, whose dust rests in our cemetery. It was under his eloquent and genial ministration the church entered upon the prosperous career it has since known. The Rev. A. J. Frost, now pastor of the University Place church, in Chicago, served as pastor during the three years following the close of Mr. Patterson's ministry, and preached his last sermon here February 9, 1862—the day the new house of worship was dedicated. The present pastor entered upon his labors here in October, 1873.

During the eleven years of its existence the church has grown from 14 members to 232. It is engaged in the work of city missions, and in its various Sunday Schools has nearly 350 pupils under instruction. A mission chapel owned by them in the First ward is already inadequate to the wants of the place, and is about to be enlarged. The church is glad to open its doors to the stranger, and extends a cordial welcome to the transient visitor as well as the new resident. The officers of the church are as follows:

Pastor—Rev. Z. Grenell, Jr.

Deacons—William H. Currey, Henry A. Gustin, Samuel Drake.

Board of Trustees—William Westover, President; C. M. Averell, Secretary; Descum Culver, Treasurer; E. B. Denison, Henry A. Gustin.

Trinity Episcopal Church.

Trinity Protestant Episcopal church, of Bay City, owed its establishment first to the Fitzhugh family, Mr. W. D. Fitzhugh having been the earliest leader in the Society, and his wife the first communicant. Israel Catlin and Col. Henry Raymond were also active in the organization. The first corporation was made March 4, 1854, by Henry Raymond, Israel Catlin, Daniel Burns, John Drake, George E. Smith, E. S. Catlin, J. S. Barclay, B. B. Hart, Henry Young, C. Munger, H. H. Alvord, H. H. Chapman and James Hays. The first services were conducted in 1850, by Rev.(deacon) Joseph Adderly, missionary at Saginaw City. Next came Rev. Daniel B. Lyon, from the same place, and held services about half a dozen times up to 1852. The first regular services were by Rev. Voltaire Spaulding, who became a missionary to this whole region, with headquarters at Saginaw City. From June, 1858, the parish was without a pastor for nearly two years. In 1860 the church edifice of wood, which had been erected on the best of the church sites reserved in the original plat, was dedicated by the Rt. Rev. S. A. McCoskry, and in May of the same year Rev. Edward Magee took charge of the parish, giving it every other Sunday, and receiving $300 per year as salary. Next year Mr. Magee devoted his entire time to this parish. His ministry of a year and a half shows a record of 14 baptisms, six confirmations, one marriage and two burials. The number of communicants at this time was 20. For a year after this date, or until Nov. 24, 1862, the parish was again vacant, and then Rev. Gilbert B. Haven came to its charge. During his ministry seven were confirmed, and ten were received from abroad, making the number of communicants August 1, 1863, about 37. Rev. A. M. Lewis was called to the rectorship Oct. 1, 1863. He remained two years, during which the church building was enlarged at a cost of $1,200, and 54 were baptised, 26 were confirmed, seven were married, and there were 13 burials. From abroad, 24 were received into the church, making the number of communicants 65. On the 19th of January, 1866, the Rev. Fayette Royce was called to the rectorship, entered upon the duties at the latter end of the March following, and resigned Nov. 1, 1868.

Rev. John Wright became rector April 11, 1869. The church had previously undergone a third extension at an expense of $2,100. Gas had been introduced, the chancel enlarged, a library room added, and the interior of the building thoroughly renovated. The expense was paid mainly by the Ladies' Aid Society, which raised in one year $1,200. In the latter pert of the year 1871, the Vestry granted the rector an extended vacation for the purpose of making a tour through Europe and the Holy Land. He was absent from January 1, 1872, to Oct. 1, of the same year. The Rev. R. McMurdy, L. L. D., officiated for six months of this time. The rector resumed his duties on the first Sunday in October. During this year a mission was established at Wenona, under the charge of Mr. George A. Cooke, as Lay Reader. October 20, 1872, the Rector organized Trinity Chapel, in the Seventh ward of the city, formerly known as Portsmouth. Three other missions were organized, at Banks, McEwanville and Essexville, making in all five missions supported by Trinity church. Oct. 12, 1873, the Rev. Lewis L. Rogers entered upon his duties as missionary at these missions. He resigned all connection with them pior to Oct. 1, 1874. On Sunday, January 18, 1874, a new organ was used for the first time in divine service. The instrument was built by Steer & Turner, of Wessfield, Mass., at a cost of $3,150.

The Rev. Mr. Wright resigned January 25, 1874, and removed to Boston, Mass. During his encumbency "Trinity Church Record," a parish publication, was issred bi-monthly. He was succeeded in the rectorship by the Rev. Geo. P. Schetky, D. D., on the 21st of June, 1874. The Rev. J. E. Jackson received an appointment as missionary, and entered upon his duties Oct. 11, 1874. Besides the present edifice and valuable lots on Washington street, the church possesses a number of lots with a comfortable rectory of the northwest corner of Grant and Center streets, upon which it is contemplated a handsome church edifice will at no very distant day be erected.

At Wenona a parochial organization has been effected, under the name of "St. Paul's church." The Rev. Mr. Jackson has become the rector. A neat frame edifice has been raised and enclosed upon lots presented by Mr. and Mrs. H. W. Sage. A similar movement is contemplated at Portsmouth. The residence of the Rev. Mr. Jackson is at Salzburg. The present number of communicants belonging to the parish is about 400; Sunday-school teachers 23; pupils 164. The Vestry is composed as follows:

Israel Catlin, Senior Warden; Thomas Cranage, Jr., Junior Warden; John Drake, Secretary and Treasurer; Wm. Keith, Henry C. Moore, Charles C. Fitzhugh, Albert H. Van Etten. Israel Catlin, Superintendent of Sunday School; Wm. H. West, Assistant Superintendent; Thaddeus Smith, Secretary and Treasurer; John W. Thompson, Librarian; Mrs. H. V. R. Ferris, Assistant Librarian; Wm. H. West, organist of church; Dr. H. B. Landon, choir master; Thomas Bailey, Sexton.

First Presbyterian Church.

The Presbyterian Church of Bay City is the third Protestant organization in order of time effected in the place, dating from the year 1856. On the 4th day of September of that year, eight persons were united in church covenant by Rev. Lucius I. Root. The names of the eight were, Albert Miller, Mary Ann Miller, Jesse Calkins, Abigail Smith, Frances T. Root, Angeline Miller, Mary E. Trombley and Nancy M. Hart.

The first officer of the church was Albert Miller, who was chosen Deacon soon after its organization. The church was without a session till June, 1858, when Albert Miller and Scott W. Sayles were chosen ordained ruling Elders.

Mr. Root continued his ministrations from the beginning until February, 1860; but till the 17th of November, 1858, his relation to the church was that of stated supply, and his labors were, for a part of the time, divided between preaching and teaching a small school. In November, 1858, he was called and instituted as Pastor of the church by the Presbytery of Saginaw; but the relation only continued till the aforesaid Febuary, 1860, when his dismission took place. His successor in the pulpit was Rev. E. J. Stewart, who commenced his work in June, 1861, and continued until September, 1864. He was never called to the Pastorate.

During Mr. Root's ministry the congregation worshipped in a school house, and afterward in a public hall, and for awhile in the court room. Mr. Stewart's term of service, though but a little over three years, was distinguished by the erection of two church edifices. The first was built in 1861, but by some defect in its heating apparatus it went wholly aflame, on a Sabbath in February, 1862, and while the congregation gathered for worship, were looking on.

Mr. Stewart bestirred himself so vigorously that another edifice was up and dedicated on the 25th of December, 1863. This building was of wood, 40x70 feet, and with additions and changes is in use yet. It has an excellent site on Washington street, near to Tenth; and as at present enlarged is a trifle in advance as to sittings of any Protestant edifice in the city, having 116 pews, besides orchestra, with wide aisles and capable of containing over 1,000 persons. It has Lecture and Sunday School rooms 19x60 feet. The audience room is fully carpeted; the pews have upholstered backs and cushioned seats, and for the purpose of worship the room is pleasant, it being in form nearly square, and thus easy for speaking and hearing, all persons being brought near to the pulpit. The bell is not a large one, but of pleasant tone, as those from the Troy works are apt to be. It was placed in the tower in August, 1866. The church is yet without an organ, but is preparing to secure one. The lecture room was built in the autumn of 1868, and the main building was enlarged one-third in 1872.

The present pastor of the church, Rev. J. Ambrose Wight, came here from Chicago, Ill., and commenced his labors May 1st, 1865, upon a call to the pastorate. He was installed by the Presbytery of Saginaw on the 23d of November following. He has seen the following changes in the pulpit of the city during his term of nine and a half years: The Catholic Church has changed once; the Lutheran once; the Methodist five times; the Baptist three time; Episcopal three times.

The additions to the church during his ministry have been 240. With two exceptions there have been additions at each communion. The whole membership of the church is 320. The Eldership of the church consists at present of the following gentlemen: Hon. Albert Miller, chosen in 1858; Dr. George E. Smith, in 1862; W. A. Cathcart, in 1867; F. A. Bancroft, J. F. Rowen, in 1870; John L. Dolsen, in 1871, and John Haynes, Esq., in 1873. Mr. Scott W. Sayles was elected in 1858, but died in 1862. Mr. B. B. Hart was chosen in 1862 and continued to act until 1871. James L. Monroe was elected in 1862, but removed in 1867; returned and was re-elected in 1870, and served till

1873, when he removed again. James Remington was chosen in 1863, also H. D. Tomar, but both removed in 1866. Caleb Jewett was elected in 1870, but removed in 1871.

The church has had a Sabbath School from the beginning. In addition to its home school a small school was commenced at the school house on the Tuscola plank road, four miles from town, by Mr. J. Hyde Monroe, in 1866, which was maintained till 1871. The young men of the church have, at different times, assisted schools at Essexville, Kawkawlin, Salzburg, and in the south part of the city. In the year 1870, the church, in the discharge of its part of the memorial celebration of the union of the branches of the Presbyterian Church in the United States, built a chapel in the Fifth Ward of the city at a cost of $1,600. In this chapel a Sabbath School has ever since been maintained. The home school and this chapel school have in connection about 500 members.

Besides the several Sabbath services, the church maintains weekly prayer meetings. The church meeting is on Wednesday evening of each week. The young people's meeting is on Sabbath evening, an hour before service.

Roman Catholic Church.

Whether the early Jesuit Missionaries ever visited this locality in their travels through the Northwest, it would perhaps be difficult, without special investigation, to decide. As the Bay and Valley of the Saginaw must have been a well-known place of rendezvous for the Indians of the lakes, it is more than probable that it received some visits from the Jaques and Brebeufs and Marquettes, and their numerous companions. Indeed the names of the places, streams and points of land on the shores of Lakes Huron and Michigan would seem to indicate the tracks of the intrepid French Catholic Missionaries. An essay on this subject by some industrious local investigator would form a valuable and interesting chapter in the history of the Saginaw Valley, but the space at our disposal forbids any attempt at a sketch of the kind.

Previous to the erection of the present St. Joseph's Church, Bay City (Lower Saginaw, as it was then called) was visited from time to time by priests from different parts of the State, most frequently by those resident in Flint and Detroit. Among those who most frequently came here prior to 1848, were Fathers Kundig and Louis, and Father

Peter Kindekens, the Vicar General of the diocese. Between 1848 and 1852 priestly visits became more frequent. Father Monayhan, then the pastor of Flint, made frequent trips to Saginaw City, and on most occasions would get some good Frenchman or Indian to paddle him down the river to Lower Saginaw. Occasionally too, Father Joseph Kindekens, brother of the Father Peter above mentioned, and Father Kilroy, now pastor of Emmett, St. Clair County, would be assigned to the duty of visiting the Catholics of the Valley,and would be watched eagerly from the shore, as he approached in canoe or on the ice, carefully holding the pack containing his altar vestmentsand vessels. In 1848 there were eight Catholic families here, most of whom were French. By 1851 the number had increased to fourteen, besides a few young, unmarried men, who had ventured in to help prepare the lands for their future wealthy occupants. Among the "old heads" there were the Trombles, the Trudells, the Longtains and the Marsacs, and among the men of younger blood there were James L. Herbert, the brothers Cusson, William Ferris and others. I have said that most of the Catholics were Frenchmen, but what spot of earth can one look at without finding there an Irishman. Lower Saginaw at that time was no exception. Here too there were Irishmen. Osmond A. Perrott, the father of our present fellow citizen, P. J. Perrott (who was then a "broth of a boy") was then residing here, and had resided here since 1842. Also Mr. Bernard Cunningham, whose memory is revered by all the older residents of Bay City. About this time too, our present wealthy and respected fellow citizen, Mr. James Watson, moved here from Detroit, bringing with him, on his father's side, the spirit and traditions of the Kentucky riflemen, and on his mother's side the memory of the good Gabriel Richard, priest and member of Congress. In 1850-1, the Catholics of Lower Saginaw considered themselves numerous enough to attempt building a church. The munificence and forethought of the men who laid out the village plat had provided building sites for the different Christian denominations whose members might settle here. The Catholics were the first to avail of the bounty, and as the most convenient to the settled portion of the village, the site of the present St. Joseph's Church was selected. There were no architects here then, but there were many who had assisted at every "raising" that had ever occurred here, and knew just what a building needed to make it last long. The men went into the woods to chop and square the timber, and each helped to put the pieces in their places in the edifice. The men were few, however; none of them were rich then (though many of them are now) and most of them had to support families besides building churches. The work consequently progressed but slowly, so much so, that when the Rev. H. J. H. Schutjes arrived here in 1852, not much of a church was to be seen. But they had now at least at their head one who could encourage and direct them; and after some time, by his efforts and their own will, the building gradually assumed shape, and Father Schutjes was soon able to perform divine service in it. It was a long time however, before a pastoral residence was built. During this time Father S. resided sometimes in the family of Mr. Watson, and sometimes in the old pioneer hotel, the Wolverton House, and he now often speaks of the kindness and good nature of the worthy hostess Mrs. J. S. Barclay. Those were the good old primitive times of Bay City when saw-mills were few and far between, and banks and newspapers were not even in the mind of the prophet. Besides Lower Saginaw, Father Schutjes was pastor of the entire Saginaw Valley. He had to divide his time between the people at this end of the river and those in the upper towns. Every alternate Sunday he spent in Saginaw City and East Saginaw, and in the spring and fall, when the ice was bad and there were no roads, he often had great difficulty and many hair-breadth escapes, in coming to and from those places. But the growth of commerce and manufactures brought increase in population. The number of Catholics kept pace with the general prosperity, and by the year 1863 they were numerous enough to require the appointment of pastors for each of the cities of Saginaw and East Saginaw. Father Schutjes was then enabled to devote his attention to the wants of his people in Bay City. Soon the little church of St. Joseph became too small for the increasing congregation. Frenchmen came from Canada, and Irishmen came from everywhere. Besides those, there were many stalwart Hollanders and Germans, so that Father Schutjes had to speak many languages to "get along" with his people. French and English being, however, the prevailing languages in the congregation, he preached alternately in those two tongues, until the year 1867. At this period it was discovered that not one-eighth part of the congregation could get into St. Joseph's church, so it was resolved at once to commence the building of a new church.

Ground was selected on the present site of St. James church, and before the close of September of that year, the new church was dedicated, under the patronage of St. James the Apostle. This church continued under the charge of Father Schutjes until June of 1873, when he was called to Detroit to assist the Bishop in the affairs of the diocese. His place was filled by the appointment of Rev. Thomas Rafter, a native of Monroe county, in this State.

Before the departure of Father Schutjes the Catholics on the west side of the river had increased so much in number that the Bishop had ordered the setting off of that territory as a separate parish, and had appointed the Rev. M. G. Cantors as pastor, with authority to at once commence the building of a church. Father Cantors at once commenced the erection of a building to serve as a chapel until it would be convenient to build a church, and which, when the church should be built would serve as a school-house. This chapel was cempleted in the early part of 1874, and is now too small for the congregation. Father Van Stralm was appointed to the charge of St. Joseph's church, which has been, since the year 1867, devoted to the exclusive use of the French Catholics of the city. Those of all nationalities other than French, on the east side of the river, are under the charge of Father Rafter, and attend St. James church.

The Germans and Poles have, however, lately become so numerous that the Bishop has deemed it proper to set them off under pastors who speak their own languages. Accordingly the Catholics of these nationalities have lately commenced the erection of new churches, the Poles on the corner of Twenty-second and Farragut street, and the Germans on Lincoln avenue, between Eighth and Ninth. As the seating capacity of the different churches is entirely disproportioned to the number of members—only a comparatively small proportion being able to get pews to rent—the pastors can give only an approximate estimate of the actual numbers of their congregations. It is supposed that the numbers will be rather within the figures if those on the Bay City side are set down at from 5,000 to 6,000, and those on the Wenona side at from 1,500 to 2,000.

It would not be proper to close this sketch of the history of Roman Catholic matters in Bay City, without alluding to the excellent parochial school of St. James church. The erection of the building for this school was commenced by Father Schutjes, but completed by the present pastor, Father Rafter. It is built from designs by Porter & Watkins, architects, of Bay City and Buffalo, and is a very handsome frame building, divided into two stories. It is 105 feet long by 36 wide. The lower story is divided into three large class-rooms, the upper story being a hall with a movable partition in the centre so as to divide it into two class-rooms. The school was opened in September, 1873, under the charge of the Sisters of Charity, from Cincinnati, with an attendance of 120 scholars. At the close of the first year the number in attendance was nearly 400. This year it opened with an attendance on the first day of 300 scholars, and as the accommodations and the number of teachers have since been increased, it is expected the attendance will be much larger than last year. The school is graded into the three departments of primary, intermediate and grammar. The furniture and school apparatus is all of the best kind, the teachers are all ladies of the best ability and experience, and the school is of a superior character. Besides the ordinary studies the girls are taught plain and fancy needle work. A class in drawing and painting was begun at the opening of the present term, under a teacher of recognized ability. Music and singing are taught by the Sisters as a specialty, and many of the daughters of our wealthiest non-Catholic fellow-citizens are now availing themselves of their recognized ability as music teachers.

A total abstinence society, of about fifty members, is also connected with St. James church, which is in a very prosperous condition. And the ladies in the congregation, married and unmarried, are organized into several societies or sodalities, for different benevolent or religious objects.

Universalist Parish of Bay City.

This parish was organized in the year 1866, with Rev. C. P. Nash as Pastor. During this year the church edifice was built, and in January, 1867 it was dedicated. Mr. Nash remained with the parish two years, closing his pastorate in 1868. Previous to his settlement, there had been occasional preaching of this order in the city, the Rev. Mr. Tompkins, then of Midland City, preaching statedly for the term of six months or more. Sometime during the year 1869, the Rev. Mr. Folsome became the pastor for the short period of about nine months, after which the Rev. A. C. Countryman supplied the desk three months, when the parish secured the settlement of the present pastor, Rev. C. W. Knickerbacker, who commenced his labors the first of January, 1871.

The parish is not large, consisting of only about forty families and numbering about two hundred members.

Their church is a neat, comfortable wooden structure, situate on Washington street, between Eighth and Ninth. The church property is worth about six thousand dollars. The parish is free from debt and seems to be in a healthy, flourishing condition.

It has a church organization also, of about forty members, and an interesting and flourishing Sunday School with a membership of over one hundred.

Fremont Avenue M. E. Church.

This church was organized in 1864 and became an independent charge in 1868, under the pastorate of the Rev. Leman Barnes. It is in a healthy and growing condition and promises to become a strong and influential church. Its property is valued at $7,000, and the society has a membership of eighty-seven. J. M. Watrous, Wm. Daglish, Albert Miller, George H. Wolverton, Henry Richards, George Lewis, J. D. Lewis, C. W. Merrill, J. T. Miller and Wm. Campbell comprise its present official board, and Rev. J. T. Hankinson is the pastor.

Methodist Episcopal Church.

This society was organized in 1845, by Rev. George Bradley, with seven members. In 1849 Mr. Bradley commenced preparations for building a church edifice, and in 1853 his labors were crowned with success. The society has been served by the ministry as follows: 1853, Rev. J. Coggshall; 1855, Rev. S. J. Joslin; 1857, Rev. William Benson; 1859, Rev. E. Klump; 1860, Rev. J. C. Wortley; 1862, Rev. E. E. Castor; 1863, Rev. H. O. Parker; 1864, Rev. Wm. Fox; 1866, Rev. R. S. Pardington; 1868, Rev. Geo. I. Betts; 1869, Rev. J. H. Burnham; 1871, Rev. John Kelly; 1874, Rev. T. G. Potter. The growth of the church has been steady until the membership now numbers 240. The Sunday School is in a flourishing condition, having about 170 pupils. There is a Mission School in the Fifth Ward. The church property is valued at $12,000. The trustees are H. M. Bradley, L. A. Barber, F. B. Smith, S. J. Seed, E. M. Fowler, W. K. Wheat, H. G. Beach, H. Holmes and A. W. Bradley.

German Lutheran Emanuel Congregation of Bay City.

The first commencement of this society dates back to the year 1854, Rev. F. Sievers of Frankenlust, the pioneer of Lutheran ministers in this section, being the founder. By him the little flock was served in connection with St. Paul's Society at Frankenlust for a period of eleven years. In 1865 Rev. I. C. Himmler took charge of the society, then numbering about twenty voting members. In the autumn of 1867, Rev. Himmler severed his connection with the society by accepting a call to another field of labor. When he left there were about twenty-five voting members and the property of the society conisted of the lot on the northwest corner of Sixth and Madison streets, with a small church building of 18x30 feet and a school house upon it. In July, 1868, after a vacancy of nine months, the charge was filled by the present pastor, Rev. I. H. P. Partenfelder, a graduate of the Lutheran Concordia Seminary at St. Louis, Mo. The number of voting members at present is 64; the whole number of souls, children included, is over 400. In 1873, the church building having become too small, an addition 22x30 feet was made. The building is now lighted by gas, contains two bells and a pipe organ. Besides this, the society has a property on the southeast corner of Sixth and Monroe streets, two lots with a valuable parsonage and a school house upon them. The value of the whole property of the congregation may be estimated at from $9,000 to $10,000. It also supports its own school teacher, now Mr. H. Graebner. The form of church government is congregational, like that of the General Lutheran Mission Synod, whereof Emanuel congregation is a member. Rev. I. H. P. Partenfelder is pastor.

Evangelical Lutheran.

The Evangelical Lutheran Bethel congregation was organized the 31st of October, 1852, according to the present constitution given by Rev. Jul. Ehrhardt, who was the first pastor of the church. During the same year a small house of worship was built on Washington street, between Seventh and Eighth streets. After the resignation of the above named pastor, the ministers of East Saginaw and Saginaw City served here for some years, till Rev. F. W. Spindler came as permanent minister in June, 1860. He resigned in November, 1862. Rev. John Haas was his successor, and he resigned in June, 1865. His successor was the present pastor, Rev. W. Reuther, who took charge September 11th, 1865. In the spring of 1866, a new church was built and the first building was removed to the rear, behind the parsonage. The new church was dedicated June 16th, 1867. The old building was used as a parochial school, attended to by Rev. W. Reuther. In June, 1871, the church was supplied with three bells, furnished by the Buckeye Bell Foundry, at Cincinnati, Ohio. October 25th, 1871, the church building and school house were destroyed by fire. This hard misfortune induced the congregation to sell the old church ground and to buy the present place, three lots on the corner of Madison and Eighth streets. A beautiful brick church was erected on this place. The dimensions of the building are 95x42 feet, with a steeple 150 feet high, supplied with two fine-toned bells. In connection with the church a new parsonage was built as a dwelling for the pastor of the church. The new church was dedicated November 25th, 1872, by the present pastor, Rev. W. Reuther, and officer of the Evangelical Lutheran Synod of Michigan and other States, of which body the congregation is a member. The whole value of the church property is about $15,000, and the number of the members of the congregation is 110, with 550 communicants.

Fremont Avenue Baptist Church.

This society was organized in 1857, at the house of Jesse M. Braddock. This was really the first Baptist Church organized in the present limits of Bay City. At the organization it had 23 members. The present church edifice was completed in 1862. The pastors who have served the society are as follows: Revs. Handy, Cornileus, Franklin Johnson, Mr. Hooker, Mr. Robinson, R. E. Whittemore in 1868, Mr. Holmes in 1872 and Chas. Fraser in 1874. The church property is valued at $4.000. It has a membership of 60, and a Sunday School comprising 100. The trustees are Elias Stevens, Henry C. Gay and William Whipple.

German M. E. Church.

The German Methodist Episcopal Church is in a very flourishing condition. It has been in existence about 15 years. The value of the church property is $4,000. There are 110 active members and a Sunday School of 50 pupils. The present pastor, Rev. Geo. A. Reuter, is an efficient teacher of the Gospel and the large and most respectable German population are likely to sustain his ministry and make it eminently successful.

High School Building.

PUBLIC SCHOOLS.

The public schools of Bay City have reached a point of excellence which justifies the feeling of pride in them entertained by the citizens generally. A brief history of the development of the school system of the city, with some notes of the school population, the present organization, etc., we append as follows:

Up to September 25, 1865, the schools of Bay City were under control of school district number two, of the tewnship of Hampton. At the date named, the inspectors formed the "school district of Bay City," and this was regularly organized on the 2d of October following. There were 166 school sittings at that time, and the aggregate attendance was 212. The only school building was a portion of what is now the Second Ward school house, on Adams street. The amount of school taxes fixed for that year was $2,616.29. On the 4th of December, 1865, another school was opened in a rented building in the Third Ward, where there were 56 sittings and 89 pupils. In January, 1866, the School Board bought the property on the corner of Adams and Eighth streets, with the building thereon, for $3,000, and a school was opened there on the 22d of the same month, with 120 sittings.

In April of the year 1866, the project of a high school was agitated, and at several meetings held in May, the matter was fully discussed. The result was that the board was instructed to buy the high school site, which is the block bounded by Ninth, Tenth, Grant and Farragut streets. The price paid for this property was $4,400. In the October following, the site for the First Ward school building was bought for $2,400; and in November the entire block 268 was bought of James Watson for $2,800. The following year buildings were put upon these sites, and a building on Saginaw street, between Fourth and Fifth, was rented for school purposes. At this time the aggregate enrollment of pupils was 522.

March 20, 1867, the Governor approved the act of the Legislature organizing the Union school district of Bay City, and the first school board under it was chosen the succeeding month. The new buildings in the First and Fifth Wards were opened in August of this year. The census showed then a school population of 1,270. In September, 1867, the contract for the high school building, a massive three-story brick edifice, was let to George Campbell at $67,350, and on the 6th of the following May the corner-stone was duly laid. In April, 1869, schools were opened in the high school building. The census of August, 1868, showed a school population of 1,533.

The rapid growth of the school establishment continued during the years following those just mentioned, and the board was constantly taxing its means to provide adequate accommodations. During the summer of 1869, an addition was made to the Second ward building, and next year it became necessary to put an additional room on the Fifth ward branch building. In the summer of 1871 a two-story addition was made to the First ward building.

The following table shows conveniently the growth of the school population, with the enrollment in schools for those years in which a record was kept:

	School Population.	Enrollment.
1865	700	212
1866	1,063	522
1867	1,270	700
1868	1,533	1,197
1869	2,003	1,220
1870	2,102	1,822
1871	2,225	1,851
1872	..	1,833
1874	3,988	2,000

The expenditures for schools were as follows, in the years named :

For the year ending September 3, 1866	$ 3,114 89
For the year ending September 2, 1867	18,905 63
For the year ending September 2, 1868	28,048 24
For the year ending May 22, 1869	55,460 63
For year 1869, tax levied	34,200 00
For year 1870, tax levied	26,115 00
For year 1871, tax levied	26,400 00
For year 1874, tax levied	45,039 00

The amount of bonded school indebtedness in 1874 was $49,570.

On the 1st of April, 1869, the Superintendency of the Bay City schools was assumed by Prof. D. C. Scoville, who at once began a most thorough work of organization and discipline. Under his able administration the schools were graded, and by his efforts and those of his assistants, the standard was brought up to a high point. The expenditures, it will be seen, were very liberal, but the advance in the efficiency of the system was at least proportionate. The schools of the city were in the transition stage from the old district school of the township and village to the completely organized system of public instruction which the city now possesses. The importance and the excellence of the labors of Prof. Scoville during this critical period in the history of the Bay City schools cannot well be overestimated.

The present school establishment of the city consists of four wooden and two brick buildings, with 2,250 sittings. The school property is valued at $125,000. The corps of teachers numbers 35, under the superintendency of Prof. I. W. Morley, who came to this city in 1869 with Prof. Scoville, and having been engaged in the schools during the superintendency of the latter, was peculiarly fitted to succeed to the office when it became vacant in the summer of 1874, by Prof. Scoville's resignation.

The school system embraces several features of more than usual merit. Among these may be mentioned the organization of the High School, by which the superior corps of teachers in that grade is given charge of the grammar school grade in the same building, thereby securing much better instruction in the latter grade than is commonly had, while the expenses are materially lessened. The High School itself has given repeated evidence of the excellence of its work in the standing of its graduates who have gone abroad to undergo the test of other schools. Graduates of the High School are in the University of Michigan, Yale College, Cornell University, Kalamazoo Female Seminary, Evanston (Ill.) Female College, Madison (N. Y.) University, Vassar Female College, and the West Point Military Academy. At Vassar and Cornell, graduates of the Bay City High School have been admitted "without conditions," the highest compliment to the High School which could come from such a source. The High School course covers three years, and the entire course of study, from the primary grade to the High School graduation, twelve years. A mixed German and English school is one of the prominent features of the system. It is so arranged that an English teacher gives instruction half the day in that language, and a German teacher the other half in his tongue. The pupils and the studies are the same in each language, and this method of combination is found to afford many advantages and to produce the best results thus far attained.

As has been said heretofore, the public school system of the city is an object of just pride to the people, who are led to make very liberal expenditures by the good results obtained in the schools. The general charge of this great interest is confided to the following Board of Education :

President—J. D. Lewis.
Clerk—I. G. Worden.
Superintendent of Schools—I. W. Morley.
First ward—Andrew Walton, (vacancy).
Second ward—L. A. Barber, S. G. M. Gates.
Third ward—E. M. Fowler, W. K. Wheat.
Fourth ward—C. F. Gibson, I. H. Hill.
Fifth ward—H. M. Bradley, (vacancy).
Sixth ward—J. D. Lewis, Duncan McGregor.
Seventh ward—C. S. Braddock, Alex. Logan.

SPECIAL SCHOOLS.

The city cannot yet boast much of special schools, but it can be said that we are not entirely destitute of them. The State Conservatory of Music is a lately organized school, which is in a most prosperous condition, and offers unexcelled facilities for the acquirement of a thorough musical education. The Sisters of the St. James Parochial School also offer the best instruction for pupils in music.

NEWSPAPERS.

Bay City is liberally supplied with newspapers. The list comprises the following:

The Tribune, daily and weekly editions. Democratic in politics, and published by an association of prominent Democrats of the county. Subscription price for daily, 65 cents per month, delivered by carrier; $7 per year by mail. Weekly, $1.50 per year.

The Chronicle, daily and weekly editions. Republican in politics, and published by the Chronicle Association. Subscription price for daily, 60 cents per month, or $7 per year by mail. Weekly, $2 per year.

The Lumberman's Gazette, a weekly journal devoted especially to the lumber interest, the first of its class and in the enjoyment of a circulation footing up over 6,000 names. It is published by Henry S. Dow, at the subscription price of $3 per year. It is the most original and the best posted organ of the lumber trade published.

It may be said of the Bay City press generally, that it has worked up its field very thoroughly, and as a reward the papers have a much larger circulation than is usual in places of like size. The two dailies, for instance, print editions of about 800 copies, a circulation for the population wholly without a parallel in Michigan, if not, indeed, in the entire West. The Weekly Chronicle enjoys a circulation greater than any other general weekly in this section has hitherto enjoyed.

THE POLES OF BAY CITY.

About three years ago an extensive Polish emigration set in to Bay City and its adjoining territory, and it seems that those of this nationality at present in the place alone amount to 200 families. The emigration hither has been aided and encouraged greatly by the efforts of Mr. L. Daniels, the manager of the custom department in the store of F. H. Blackman & Co. Mr. Daniels has been so attentive to the wants of the newly-arrived that he is looked upon by all his country people in Bay City as their chief advisor, and to a large extent their guardian. The fact that the Polish language is spoken by none but Poles, and few of them having any knowledge of English, rendered it necessary that as soon as their numbers would justify the step, an attempt should be made to build a separate place of worship for them. This design was fostered by Mr. Daniels, and to secure the organization necessary to accomplish the object, he induced his countrymen to form themselves into a society. This association was formed on the 8th of February, 1874, with Mr. Daniels as President, each member agreeing to pay a certain sum each month to form a fund for the building of the contemplated church. But this would have taken a long time to accomplish, while in the meantime their number was increasing. Accordingly Mr. Daniels set to work to build a church at once. He procured subscriptions from most of our prominent fellow-citizens, and Mr. Wm. D. Fitzhugh, with the liberality in such matters for which he and his father and brothers are so noted, gave a site for the church consisting of eight lots on the corner of Lincoln avenue and Twenty-second street. A contract for the building of the church was let last July, to Mr. Neil Mahoney, after plans by L. A. Pratt, architect, both of this city. The building is now completed, and will be consecrated by Rt. Rev. Casper H. Borgess, Bishop of Detroit, on Sunday, the 13th of December next, (1874). The building will cost about $4,000, is a very neat and tasteful edifice, and is located on a very fine site, and convenient to those who will worship there. Mr. Daniels has had the entire control and responsibility of the work, and of providing the money for it, and his countrymen in Bay City owe him a very great debt of gratitude.

Jennison Block.

LUMBER MANUFACTURE.

The paramount interest of this city, the actual and the natural metropolis of the Saginaw region, is of course the lumber manufacture. Here are located two of the largest saw-mills in the world, those of John McGraw & Co., and H. W. Sage & Co., the latter across the river in the village of Wenona. The former of these mammoth establishments, at a recent test, cut at the rate of 800,000 feet a day, a feat entirely without a parallel in the world. The product of this single mill at the above rate of production would be worth over $11,000 each day, taking the ruling prices of this year as the standard.

The facilities for the manufacture and shipment of lumber at this point are unrivalled. The broad Saginaw river affords unlimited booming ground for the storage of logs, and in the deep channel the largest lake vessels may ply free from the dangers of sand bars, which annoy localities farther up the stream. Logs from the Cass, the Tittabawassee and their tributaries, are rafted down to the mills here at small additional expense over the cost at upper river mills, and logs from the shore streams are brought in from the bay to this, the central point of the Saginaw lumbering region. The city is well supplied with boiler and machine shops for all kinds of mill work, and the Holly water works pipes extend from one end of the town to the other, affording the best possible fire protection, and giving good facilities for filling and cleaning boilers, etc.

There are in the city proper 77 manufacturing establishments, which employ a capital of $4,086,789. Of these, 28 are saw-mills, in which are 34 circular saws, and 21 gangs. In the entire county there are 112 manufacturing establishments, employing a capital of $5,952,789. Of this total, 38 are saw-mills along the river in the immediate vicinity of Bay City. The magnitude of the operations of these saw-mills will be best shown by the following table, which exhibits the shipments of the various articles named, as reported to the custom-house here.

The exhibit is as follows:

LUMBER, ETC., SHIPPED FROM BAY CITY IN 1873.

DESTINATION.	Lumber.	Lath.	Shingles.
Buffalo	75,266,578	5,804,600	3,089,000
Tonawanda	60,968,012	1,234,000	2,486,000
Cleveland	46,392,687	8,404,000	14,726,000
Toledo	25,909,231	4,359,000	14,000
Erie	17,578,207	1,398,000	900,000
Ogdensburg	15,709,471	......	......
Detroit	7,945,494	154,000	......
Sandusky	4,476,994	1,507,000	2,200,000
Chicago	2,386,499	......	......
Oswego	1,497,000	......	......
Dunkirk	1,885,000	......	......
Ashtabula	690,000	......	......
Port Huron	225,331	......	......
Kingston	120,000	40,000	40,000
Amhertsburg	126,017	......	39,000
Fremont	150,000	107,000	......
Wyandotte	250,000	......	......
Fairport	1,457,000	281,000	518,000
Vermillion	900,000	100,000	......
Cape Vincent	207,660	......	......
Clayton	130,000	......	......
Monroe	248,000	......	......
Collins Bay	110,000	......	......
Black River	533,280	428,000	......
Grand River	243,788	....	......
Total	265,408,193	23,816,925	24,012,000

Computing the value of these articles at the prices which prevailed during the year of their shipment, we have the following result:

Lumber - - - - - - - - -	$3,715,712
Lath - - - - - - - - - -	41,678
Shingles - - - - - - - - -	84,042
A total of - - - - - - - - -	$3,841,432

To carry this vast product to market would require not less than one thousand vessels of more than the average size of our lake craft.

But it should be borne in mind, in estimating the magnitude of the lumber business of this city, that no account is made in the above calculation, of a considerable quantity of lumber, etc., which was not reported at the custom house here, nor of the shipments by rail. An allowance of fifteen per cent. of the above aggregate would not be too large for such shipments. We should then have a total of lumber for the year of over 306,219,000 feet, and its value would be not less than $4,273,068, while the total value of the three articles above named would be $4,417,645.

We have given, however, only the shipments by lake and the estimated shipments by rail from the mills in this city and along the river banks contiguous thereto. Large as the aggregate is, it does not show the total business of the section which is immediately tributary to Bay City. There are many mills located along railroads, the owners of which do all their business and reside in this city, purchase their supplies here, etc. The business of these mills is as much a part of the business of Bay City as any other. Such are the mills along the line of the Jackson, Lansing & Saginaw railroad northward from this point, which produced in 1873 a little over 50,000,000 feet of lumber, all of which was shipped by rail. These mills also produced over 15,000,000 shingles. The total value of their products was therefore not less than $750,000.

SALT MANUFACTURE.

The vast salt basin which underlies the Saginaw Valley at a depth ranging from 600 to 1,000 feet affords an exhaustless source of wealth. Great as have been the results of the development of this industry hitherto, there are unmistakable indications that thus far the workings have been only upon the surface of the mine which lies below the bottom of the deepest wells. The immense deposit of rock salt from which the brine used in our salt works must come, has not been touched in the Valley wells, and it remains for future enterprise to sink wells to that bed of pure salt and obtain a brine stronger and purer than any yet got. The existence of this bed of rock salt has been proved by borings in Huron county to the east, and in the shore counties to the north. Our Valley manufacturers have been satisfied thus far with the very excellent brine obtained from what is known as the salt rock.

There are in and about Bay City 27 salt making establishments, three being new ones built in 1874. The others produced in 1873 a little more than 352,000 barrels of salt, which sold at $1.40 per barrel as an average, making the value of the entire product about $490,000. The capital invested in these works is about $100,000.

Most of the production comes from steam blocks, in which the evaporation is procured by the use of exhaust steam from the engines which drive saw-mills. The expense of fuel is thus reduced to the minimum, as were the steam not used in the salt manufacture, it would be suffered to escape without further service. This mode of manufacture has practically superseded all others, because of the economy of fuel above noted. This economy is such as to enable our manufacturers to successfully compete under the present low tariff with the Canadian makers, though the latter have the advantage of less expensive labor, with equally good brine.

The brine of the Saginaw wells stands at 96 and 98 by the salometer, and is freer from troublesome impurities—"bitter waters," the operatives call them—than the brine of most other localities. These impurities only require greater care in the manufacture, and with that they do not injure the salt. The system of inspection, which is under the supervision of an officer appointed by the Governor, Dr. S. S. Garrigues, is very strict in its requirements, and under it the salt of this Valley has won a high repute in the markets of the country. An especial feature with our salt manufacture is the excellence of the packages in which it is sent to market. Having the best and cheapest material ready to their hands, the makers here have shown a commendable pride in shipping their salt in the best possible shape.

The cost of a first-class steam salt block, to run in connection with a saw-mill, and to produce from 80 to 100 barrels of salt in a day, is from $12,000 to $16,000. This includes the well and all machinery ready for operation. The cost of making a barrel of salt in one of these blocks is variously estimated at from 50 to 80 cents, including the barrel in which it is packed. Even at $1.25 per barrel it will be seen that the manufacturer has a fair margin.

The field for this enterprise, as we have remarked, is exhaustless.

Anywhere along the river the brine may be found, no boring having yet failed to get a good supply. The last two years have shown a large increase in the number of salt-making establishments in this city and vicinity, and in their product. Most of the saw-mills now have a steam salt block attached.

STAVES, OAK TIMBER AND HOOPS.

The trade in oak staves and oak timber has grown to enormous proportions within a few years. It is one of the sources of wealth which was entirely overlooked during the first years of the marvelous development of the pine lumber business. Thus we find the shipments from the entire Saginaw river in 1869 amounted to only 765,000 cubic teet of oak timber, and 3,700,000 staves, while from the port of Bay City alone there were shipped last year 4,187,920 cubic feet of oak timber, and 6,480,898 staves. We give below a table showing the shipments of the three articles named in 1873, with their destination:

TO	Staves.	Sq. Oak.	Hoops.
Buffalo	4,008,523	....	8,499,800
Tonawanda	62,000	2,239,000	2,258,000
Sandusky	....	....	8,000
Oswego	....	....	2,104,000
Kingston	2,882,375	1,582,170	....
Cleveland	....	....	460,000
Clayton	31,000	192,500	....
Collins Bay	7,000	174,200	....
Total	6,990,898	4,187,870	13,329,800

The value of the above, at the prices which prevailed at the time of shipment would be :

Staves	$ 583,200
Oak Timber	837,400
Hoops	79,974
A total of	$1,500,574

PLANING MILLS, WOODEN PIPE WORKS, ETC.

There is no branch of industry in this section, and few indeed in any other, so inviting to the capitalist as the finer working of the wealth of pine and other timber. The first idea of those who became engaged in business here was to start out the pine trees in any shape so as to get them out of the river as fast as possible. Logs, long timber, or rough timber in rafts—any way would do so that it was speedy. Now, however, when it begins to be apparent that, vast as are the remaining resources of our forests, it is still possible to reach the end of them, men are thinking of other things than reckless slaughter of the pines. The enormous gains of the intermediate dealers, and the small profits which come to the manufacturer of rough lumber when the times are bad, have turned attention to finer manipulations as a surer source of profit. The advantages for this finer work are here equal to the best to be found anywhere. Some remarks concerning the cheapness of fuel, shipping facilities, etc. will be found in another part of this work, and are pertinent to the subject now treated of.

Considerable progress has already been made in the direction of a finer manipulation of our lumber, and the success of the establishments which have been started affords greater encouragement for the future. There are now in operation in Bay City and its immediate vicinity 17 planing machines, distributed through ten establishments. The largest number is found in the mammoth mill of John McGraw & Co., where there are five. These planers will work from 15,000 to 20,000 feet of lumber per day. Say the average is 18,000 feet, and we have a capacity for turning out planed lumber of over 300,000 feet per day.

There are three establishments which have, beside planers, other kinds of wood-working machinery, such as moulding and mortising machines, scroll saws, etc., and generally whatever is needed for the manufacture of ornamental wood for buildings, doors, sash, blinds, etc.

The business of these establishments, as has been stated above, is steadily prosperous and increasing. The best informed and far-seeing lumbermen look forward to the time when not a log nor a rough board will go from the Saginaw river, but the manufacture will be finished here, where it can be done to the best advantage.

There is located in Bay City a manufactory which is the only one of its kind in the country. This is the Northwestern Gas and Water Pipe Works, where the Wyckoff pipe is made. This pipe is a combination of iron bands and wood peculiarly treated and manufactured by machinery designed especially for the purpose. The pipes are cut out of solid logs by cylinder saws, two or three pipes being obtained from a log of large size. This factory employs from 60 to 75 men, and in 1874 received a single order from a Michigan city amounting to $90,000 worth of pipe.

The pipe is used for both water and gas, and being thoroughly tested, has been found very serviceable and durable. About seven miles of it are laid for water in this city, and no trouble has been found with it in any instance; it is even safer than iron in some respects.

Another special industry in Bay City is a tub and pail factory, which during the dull times succeeding the panic of 1873 was full of orders, and finding a ready market for all its products. It is known as the Bay City Wooden Ware Works. This establishment has had great inducements offered to remove its manufactory to other cities, but the advantages here are not easily overcome.

SHIPBUILDING.

No point on the great lakes offers better facilities for shipbuilding than Bay City. The quality of the oak timber to be found here is famed throughout the country, and it is even sought in the foreign markets, large quantities being sent to England. The timber is very large, and the quality of the best. Tamarack, a very useful and desirable timber for certain purposes in shipbuilding, is here to be had of sufficient size for upper-deck beams, etc. Pine sticks for masts and spars are cut in the neighboring woods and hauled direct into the yards, the same being true of the oak and other varieties used. It follows that the best obtainable material is to be had here at less cost than elsewhere. These facts have induced the establishment on the river of several extensive yards, from which have been launched some of the largest and finest vessels now afloat.

Among these yards may be mentioned that of Ballentine & Co., opposite the northern limits of Bay City, which is furnished with a steam saw-mill and every facility for the construction of vessels. This yard is now represented in the lake marine by the large steamships *D. Ballentine* and *C. J. Kershaw*, the mammoth schooner *A. B. Moore*, and numerous other fine craft.

Capt. Davidson's ship-yard is located on the west side of the river, nearly opposite the centre of the city. It has also a steam saw-mill and all needed appliances. The large steamship *James Davidson* was launched from this yard in the spring of 1874, and is one of the finest on the lakes.

Just above the last named yard is Hitchcock's yard, where were built last winter two barges for the lumber trade on an entirely new principle. The sides are of squared pine timber, securely bolted together, instead of the usual frames and planking.

The Saginaw river ship-yards turned out in 1873 no less than 22 craft of various kinds. Last winter, owing to the panic and the consequent depression in all business, the same yards furnished but seven new craft of the larger classes, though there were several tugs and like smaller craft turned out. The vessels built, however, were all of the best class, and four of them are of the largest now afloat on the lakes. The value of the product of the shipyards in 1873 was estimated at $600,000; for 1874 it was about $400,000.

We note some of the conditions favorable to the business at this point. Oak timber can be purchased in the river for from $175 to $200 per 1,000 cubic feet, or it can be bought on the stump, convenient for cutting and hauling to the yard, for $60 per 1,000 cubic feet. Spar timber can be had of any required dimensions, at reasonable prices, and all stuff for decks, upper works, etc., can be procured from first hands, or manufactured from the log on the spot. Tamarack for knees and lighter beams can be had at little more than the cost of cutting and hauling. The wages of mechanics in the ship-yards last winter averaged $2.50 per day, with common labor proportionately less.

IRON MANUFACTURE.

The subject of iron manufacture at this point has been alluded to in other parts of this work, in connection with the discovery of a good coal supply in such a location as to enable it to meet here the ores of Lake Superior to advantage. There are already, however, some very plain advantages for the trade here, among which may be mentioned the demand for a great variety of work in the mills and on the various kinds of craft navigating the adjacent waters. To supply this demand Bay City has now five machine shops, one of which is but just started, and is on a plan more extensive than any similar concern this side of Detroit. This is the Industrial Works, which will be enlarged to include facilities for all kinds of mill and engine work, and eventually, doubtless, a car factory. The company is abundantly able to carry out all its plans, and already has fine brick buildings for the works.

The other iron working establishments of the city are two machine shops beside the one specially mentioned above, and several boiler shops. All of these find plenty of employment, mostly in work for this immediate vicinity.

RAILROAD FACILITIES.

The railroad facilities of Bay City are the growth of but a very few years. The first line laid was an extension of the Flint & Pere Marquette. That road then run to Holly, there connecting with the Detroit & Milwaukee road to Detroit. Since that time the F. & P. M. company have laid a new line from Holly to Toledo, and extended their road west of the Saginaw river to Ludington, on the shore of Lake Michigan.

The Jackson, Lansing & Saginaw railroad runs down the west bank of the Saginaw river, and crosses to this city by a bridge. This road is now extended northward on its way to the Straits of Mackinaw, to a point about 100 miles from Bay City. It opens up a fine pine-bearing country, aud much valuable farming land. Southward, it affords shipping facilities to Chicago and all points west and south.

The Detroit & Bay City railroad was completed in 1873 and opened to travel in the fall of that year. It is nearly an air line to Detroit, passing through the pine lands of Lapeer county, and the rich farming country of Tuscola, Lapeer and Oakland counties. At Detroit the road has immediate connections with the Michigan Central and the Canadian roads. At Lapeer it crosses the Port Huron & Lake Michigan railway, forming a connection for Port Huron, on the St. Clair river.

A road bed has been graded from Bay City to Midland, where it will intersect the Flint & Pere Marquette road, making a nearly direct route from this city across the State to Lake Michigan. A new road, however, is in progress from the Grand Rapids region, which will connect at Midland with the road to this city, making the most direct route across the State from east to west.

A road up the bay shore to the north, and one along the opposite shore to tne northeast, will probably be among the projects of the near future. The roads already built and in progress make Bay City the railroad centre of the Valley. The facilities of deep water navigation at this point must determine the route of any new enterprise in favor of Bay City as against any point further up the river.

The roads now built afford many facilities for the shipment of munufactures to all parts of the country, east, west or south.

AGRICULTURE.

The agricultural resources of this section are as yet in their very infancy. The prairie lands of the west have attracted settlers who were discouraged by the heavy growth of timber which must be cut off the land in this vicinity before it can be made ready for the farmer. Yet for the settler of limited means the wooded lands of Michigan are decidedly preferable to the western prairies. Here he can be in the receipt of an income from the moment he begins work on his land, for the timber with which it is covered is valuable for many purposes. He can build himself a house at as small expense as he chooses, having all the material ready to his hand. He may work during the summer on his farm, and in the winter get good wages in the lumber woods at a time when he has no farm work to do. On the prairie he must buy at extravagant prices lumber for every use, and set still in the winter and eat up what he has earned during the summer. He will find here the best market for all varieties of farm products, and need not burn corn for fuel because it will not pay for hauling to market. He will get here the most remunerative prices for his farm crops. Hay has often sold in the late winter for from $30 to $40 per ton on our streets, and potatoes run from $1.50 per bushel upward before the new crop comes on.

These advantages have of late seemed to become better understood than before, and the consequence has been a very rapid increase in agricultural pursuits during the last two or three years. The farmer may choose almost any soil that pleases him, from the hard clay and heavy bottom land to the light warm soil of the higher ridges. Michigan pine is always interspersed with hardwoods, and what are called pine ridges are by no means barren drifts of sand, but good soil, on which fine wheat crops may be raised. The vegetables from some of the Saginaw Valley lands have on late occasions won premiums at the State fairs.

The State census of 1874 shows that there were in the ground in Bay county in the spring of that year 668 acres of wheat, against 513½ acres harvested in 1873. The amount of the wheat crop in 1873 was 11,042 bushels, or a little over 21½ bushels to the acre. Other farm crops, etc., for 1873, were as follows: Corn 28,653 bushels; other grains, 23,775 bushels; potatoes, 61,422 bushels; hay, 5,816 tons; pork sent to market, 8,192 lbs; and of wool only 793 lbs. The dairy product is represented by a result of 55,655 lbs. of butter sent to market, and the live stock returned foots up 5,031 animals.

There are many fine farms along the lines of plank road running east and west from the river, but the settlement of the country even in the immediate vicinity of the city is not general. There are therefore valuable lands to be had at low prices, within almost walking distance of as good a market as the State affords. We mention the farm of Nathan Knight, in the township of Hampton, three or four miles from this city, as an example of what may be done by the intelligent agriculturist. Mr. Knight's crops are luxuriant in growth and yield, and never fail. The fine market farm of E. B. Denison, on the west side of the river, supplies this market with many of its early vegetables, as well as later crops. Along the line of the plank road to Tuscola county, there may be seen as fine farming lands as can be found anywhere, sufficiently rolling for all purposes, without being hilly or cut up by ravines.

Three plank roads run off into the country from this city, giving easy access to market at all seasons. One of these roads strikes off in an easterly direction to Tuscola county, a fine agricultural region, already well developed. The second runs westward, crossing the river by a bridge and making off toward the county seat of Midland county, also a good agricultural section. The third follows in the main the course of the shore northward toward Kawkawlin, and when completed will tap an excellent farming country.

As the traveler proceeds northward along the shore of Saginaw bay, a still greater variety of land is found. Back from the shore at a distance of a few miles, the land rises rapidly, until at the crossing of the Au Gres river by the Jackson, Lansing & Saginaw railroad, the altitude is several hundred feet above that of Bay City. Here is a diversified country, watered abundantly by the purest streams, which never freeze over in winter and never become warm in summer, and in which the specked trout and the famous grayling spcrt in countless numbers.

An account of the varieties of timber indigenous to the lands of this section will be found elsewhere in this work, under the head of "Undeveloped Resources."

Watson Block.

TRIBUTARY COUNTRY.

The natural position of Bay City, at the head of deep water navigation on the Saginaw river, is one of very great advantage. A glance at a map of the State will show that Saginaw bay cuts into the lower peninsula until it reaches a point far in toward its geographical centre. It is by many miles the farthest inland from the general outline of the State of any point which is to be reached by deep water navigation. The advantage of such a position is too obvious to need comment.

As a result of this position, Bay City finds a large extent of territory about her which is naturally and necessarily tributary to her markets. This territory is generally very new and little settled as yet, but it is all good land, and upon much of it there stands as fine timber as can be found on the continent. The pine lumber business of the district known as "The Shore," extending from the mouth of the Saginaw northward to Thunder Bay, a distance of about 140 miles by the steamer route, is already very large. The young and rapidly growing villages of Alpena, East Tawas, Tawas City, Harrisville, Au Sable, Alabaster and some others, are stretched along the line of shore, and find their only regular connection with the country in general and its markets, by the steamers which ply between Bay City and the Shore ports.

At some time in the not far-distant future, a line of railway will doubtless run northward from this city, touching all the Shore points and affording the inhahitants of that region the facilities of communication in winter which they now enjoy only during the summer months of navigation, but which their business needs at all times. Back of this shore is a very fine farming country, which is being rapidly settled by thrifty immigrants.

To the east and northeast there is a fine stretch of country which finds its nearest market at Bay City, and will in time have a line of railway to that point. The agricultural interests of Tuscola and Lapeer counties are already well developed, and the lately-completed Detroit & Bay City railway brings the trade of that region to this point, its natural market.

Westward from Bay City is the district about Midland, and a little south of west, at a distance of 30 to 50 miles, is the rich farming country of Gratiot, Isabella, Montcalm and other counties. all to be brought into direct and easy communication with us by the railroad now well under way from this point west across the State.

The Flint & Pere Marquette gives intercouse with the south in one direction, and the Jackson, Lansing & Saginaw in another—both running through a fine country, interested in the great industries which centre in Bay City.

SPORTS OF THE COUNTRY.

There is no section of the country so near railways and steamboats and all the accessories of civilization, which still affords the sportsman such magnificent fields and such tempting prizes in the way of hunting and fishing as Northern Michigan offers. A four hours' ride from Detroit brings the sportsman to Bay City, and a further journey of about the same duration by rail or steamer, takes him to the unbroken native forest, where may be found all the animals which have inhabited this country since its discovery. He may, if he chooses, content himself with wild duck or a deer chase; or, if he be more venturesome, the black bear invites a trial of his skill and nerve, and the wolf and the wildcat are ready to soothe his slumbers at night with their kind attentions.

The rivers of this section abound with some of the finest fish the continent affords, and the waters of Saginaw bay and Lake Huron teem with them. To the northward, three or four hours' ride by rail brings one to streams in which are found trout, grayling and other game fish. The Au Sable river runs from a plateau six or seven hundred feet above the level of the lake, and along its wooded course over rocks and down steep rapids the magnificent grayling waits for the angler. A trip of forty or fifty miles down this stream, in a canoe or boat, gives opportunity for as fine sport as can be wished. In the Saginaw river, the bay and the lake are bass, pickerel, etc., in great numbers. Trolling for these prizes is exciting sport.

All about the newer portions of the country around Bay City, deer abound and are hunted in various ways. Wild turkeys and geese, ducks and all the smaller game are plentiful and easily to be had. Along the many small bays on the east shore of Saginaw bay, and on the prairie lands cut by bayous on the Saginaw river, ducks are found in large numbers, and afford excellent sport with boat or dog.

Hunting parties from the older States not unfrequently visit this section for a camp-out in the woods and a week's hunting. As before remarked, the near vicinity of these native wilds to the comforts of civilization makes them wonderfully attractive. The sportsman reaches them without fatiguing journeys, and when tired of his sport returns in a few hours to his home or a first-class hotel.

SUMMER RESORTS.

In the immediate vicinity of, or easily to be reached from Bay City, are a number of summer resorts, which are already popular and are destined to become still more so. Perhaps the chief of these is Mackinaw, which is reached from this city by as fine a line of side-wheel passenger steamers as can be found on any of the lake routes. Mackinaw island is a point of great interest on account of the novel natural attractions, the fine salubriousness of the air, and the unexcelled facilities for fishing, boating, etc. The accommodations for visitors are good.

There are several points on Saginaw bay which must soon be favorite resorts. Among these is Jerome's Island, near Wild Fowl Bay, where there are already accommodations for small parties. The bay just mentioned also affords numerous attractions, especially for sportsmen, the duck hunting and fishing being unusually good.

Otsego Lake is a point on the Jackson, Lansing & Saginaw railway about four hours' ride northward from Bay City. The air and water here are much admired, and the point is a favorite one for picnic parties. Boating and fishing in the lake are among the pastimes indulged in.

Southward, we have on the line of the Detroit & Bay City railway, about two hours and a half from this city, the beautiful inland watering place of Orion Lake. Here are all the accommodations usually to be found in the midst of a thriving and intelligent rural population, and the grounds about the lake have received considerable improvement to fit them for visitors.

The somewhat famous magnetic springs of St. Louis are distant about three hours by rail from this city. Hotels and all needed conveniences are provided at these springs, the waters of which have effected some very remarkable cures. At Midland there is a similar spring, with a cure attached, and mineral waters are found at Alpena, on the shore north of Bay City.

Beside the points named, nearly all the beautiful inland lakes of Michigan are easily accessible by rail from Bay City, and all points on the great lakes are reached by regular lines of passenger steamers.

Munger Block.

UNDEVELOPED RESOURCES.

Much as has been accomplished in the development of the vast sources of wealth in our pine forests, it is dwarfed almost to insignificance by comparison with the undeveloped resources of this region in general and of Bay City in particular. The branches of industry for which there are peculiarly favorable conditions here, are multitudinous. The cheapness of fuel is the most prominent advantage, perhaps, to the stranger, but there are others not less valuable. Among these we may enumerate the facilities for shipment by lake and by several competing lines of railway, the same agencies also bringing to our docks supplies and material from all parts of the country. Mention should be made likewise of the great extent of river front, affording sites for manufactories of any kind, with water and railroad communication.

It may be said generally that any manufacture into which wood enters may be carried on here to unusual advantage. The refuse from sawmills has been a burden and an expense, and mill men have been thereby prompted to engage in salt making simply as a means of utilizing and getting rid of their refuse fuel. All kind of wood-working concerns make more or less fuel in their refuse, but a big saw-mill turns out vastly more than can be burned up in its great furnaces.

The forests of this section of Michigan are boundlessly rich in timber of almost all the domestic varieties, and it is to be had at this point for little more than the cost of cutting and hauling. Many varieties are found here in greater excellence than at any other point of which we have knowledge. It is not too much to say that the well known unequalled excellence of the white pine of this region is but a fair sample of all the other woods hereabouts, as compared with the products of other sections.

The pine timber will be found treated of in the article on lumber manufacture. We note now some of the other valuable varieties of timber in this region.

OUR NATIVE WOODS.

OAK.

The country about the Saginaw Valley abounds in oak of several kinds. The shipbuilder finds here what is pronounced to be the finest timber for his purpose to be obtained on the lakes. The prices paid for this timber were as follows in 1874: Stumpage (uncut timber) $60 per thousand cubic feet; manufacturing into square timber, $45 per thousand cubic feet; and to haul to a stream for loading or use, at the rate of say $60 per thousand cubic feet for a ten mile haul. These prices would make the cost of the square timber in the river $165 per thousand. The price paid here for shipping to Canadian ports, to go thence to Liverpool, has ranged this season from $180 to $220 per thousand according to quality and size of the sticks.

Red and other varieties of oak are also abundant, and are used in the manufacture of staves, etc.

CEDAR.

There are in various localities hereabouts, and especially along the bay shore to the east, large quantities of white cedar. This wood makes the best of fence posts, and is extensively cut for that purpose. The posts sell on the docks here at from 10 to 12 cents apiece. Of late, the cedar trees ranging in diameter from six to fifteen inches, have been cut up into blocks for street paving, and they are found to answer that purpose admirably. The well known enduring qualities of the cedar recommend it strongly for this use. Of course the vast supplies of this wood hereabouts might be utilized for any purpose for which that wood is usually employed elsewhere.

TAMARACK.

The growth of tamarack which is found in this section is unusually large, and the wood is therefore more than commonly valuable for several special uses. Notable among these uses is that for ship timber. The tamarack is as stiff and almost as strong as oak, while it is much lighter. This makes it especially desirable for deck timbers in upper decks, and it has of late been used in some of the finest vessels built in this locality. Its serviceableness in shipbuilding has long been known.

HEMLOCK.

There are vast tracts of land throughout Northern Michigan, which yield large quantities of hemlock. This wood is said to possess in a peculiar degree the tannin principle, which alone makes it valuable for tanners' use. Except for the manufacture of an extract for curing leather, the hemlock has yet been little touched, though the forests afford very handsome trees of an unusual size.

BEECH.

Beech is one of the most abundant of our native woods, many large tracts being almost entirely covered with it. As yet it has not been utilized for any of the manufactures into which it may profitably enter.

MAPLE.

This wood is profusely interspersed with beech in many sections hereabouts. Curl and birdseye maple abound in the country northward, and have been cut only to a very limited extent for manufacturing purposes. Its value is well known for ornamental furniture, yet land which affords it in great quantities may be bought for from $3 to $6 per acre, not many miles from this city, and easily accessible by rail.

BIRCH.

Like the beech, the birch of this section is unusually large and fine. The yellow birch is found in large quantities, and is a wood of well known value in the manufacture of furniture.

WHITE ASH.

White ash, which is so extensively used in the manufacture of handles for various tools and implements, and for furniture, is one of the commonest of our woods. It may be had here for from $20 to $25 per thousand feet, of excellent quality and affording as handsome material of the kind as could be wished for. This wood is elsewhere extensively used for wagon and carriage work, and is, in short, one of the most useful of our native woods. Any manufacture into which it enters could be established here to the best possible advantage so far as regards the procurement of raw material at low prices.

HICKORY.

The forests of this part of the State afford a great deal of hickory of the various kinds. It has not yet been put to any use except as fire-wood, though the quality and size of the trees should suggest some better use of them.

BLACK ASH.

This timber is found in the country about Bay City in great abundance. It is chiefly worked for hoops, the greater part of which are used here in the manufacture of salt barrels. The hoop maker pays from 50 cents to $1 for his timber on the stump; he hires men to split or rive the hoops for $2.25 per thousand, and he sells them to the salt manufacturer for $5.50 per thousand. Out of this apparent profit he has to provide for felling the trees, hauling them to the place of manufacture, and for hauling the hoops to the consumer. The net profit under the above conditions is from $1 to $1.50 per thousand, providing the timber is cut at a reasonable distance from the point of delivery. A good day's work for one man is the riving out of 1,000 hoops from the log. On an ordinary haul, a team will draw the logs for 10,000 hoops in half a day, and in the other half will deliver 20,000, or two loads of hoops at two or three times the distance. The black ash trees found in this vicinity yield from 500 to 7,000 or more hoops each.

ELM.

There is an abundance of elm in the forests of this section. Of late it has been cut for hoops and staves, which it produces of good quality, and has the advantage of being easily worked.

There is some rock elm hereabouts, but the quantity is not great, the common variety prevailing.

BUTTERNUT.

On some of the bottom lands along the streams which empty into the bay north of this city, the butternut is found in considerable quantity. Much of this timber, however, which is valuable for furniture, has been wantonly cut and left to rot on the ground.

SOFT WOODS.

The soft woods of this section, other than the different varieties of pine, do not occupy a prominent place as material for lumbering operations. There is in the country to the north a large quantity of poplar, and there is some basswood all about this region. Few better localities than this could be found for the manufacture of paper pulp from wood, the poplar being peculiarly well adapted to this use, and being found in great abundance in the region mentioned. By the new patent process, this manufacture is much simplified, and thousands of acres of material could be had here for a very little amount of capital.

COAL.

It has long been known that the centre of the coal field of Michigan lies in the vicinity of the head of the Saginaw river. Outcroppings of coal are found in the country on almost every side of Bay City. At Corunna, thirty or forty miles south, coal mines have been opened and are in successful operation. Along the Cass river, east and southeast from Bay City, the outcroppings of coal are often found. This is at a distan of not more than twenty miles from this point. The opinion has long prevailed that at the proper depth below the Saginaw river valuable coal strata would be found. The idea is strengthened by the fact that nearly every boring for salt has passed through coal seams of greater or less thickness, though we believe none have been noted of a thickness that would be called a paying one. As it is well known, however, that the coal deposits are not of uniform thickness over large areas, but are rather the fillings of gulches and valleys in the old rocks, the experience of the salt well borers is by no means discouraging. There is, on the contrary, every reason to believe that somewhere between the thin outcropping veins along the Cass river and the Saginaw at this point, coal seams will be found of requisite thickness to reward the miner. Whenever this is done,iron manufacture in all its forms will become one of the great industries of this region. The Lake Superior ore can be brought here cheaper than to any of the present manufacturing points, and if coal is also here, the great essentials for profitable manufacture are certain. The abundance of material for charcoal has already induced the location of an extensive furnace on the east bay shore by capitalists from Cleveland, that city of iron works.

PLASTER AND LIME.

At various points along the bay shore there are valuable beds of limestone, which have as yet been hardly touched. At Wild Fowl Bay there are very extensive limestone beds, which only need development to be profitable. At White Stone Point, on the west side of the bay, there is a magnificent bed of limestone, which lies in the best imaginable position for easy quarrying and shipment. This has already been worked to some extent, and with the return of general prosperity, it will doubtless be fully developed. A test of the stone from this quarry establishes its superior excellence, ann the products of thebed are available with far less than the usual amount of labor in dressing.

At Alabaster, some miles north of Bay City, on the bay shore, there are valuable beds of plaster, which have been worked extensively by Smith, Bullard & Co. At Wenona, opposite Bay City, they have a mill for grinding the plaster, whence it is shipped in barrels to various markets. The analysis of this plaster shows several points wherein it excels the Grand Rapids and Sandusky products. The shipments of the firm named for 1873 aggregated 21,600 tons of rock plaster, and 12,400 bbls. of ground plaster.

It may be mentioned here that beside the limestone above noted, the shore of Huron county, east of Bay City, affords most excellent sandstone for building purposes—harder than the famous Ohio sandstone—which awaits only the necessary capital to open quarries. On the Cass river, also, valuable stone has been found, one variety of which is an unstratified soft stone, well adapted to furniture uses, being eaily worked, capable of high finish, and well adapted to the process of marbleizing.

Residence of Hon. James Shearer.

NOTEWORTHY CITIZENS.

Of the great number of noteworthy citizens who have materially contributed to the advancement of Bay City during the past few years, the following, who are not named among the pioneers, are especially deserving of mention: James Shearer, President of the First National Bank and President of the Saginaw Valley Lumbermen's Association; William Westover, President of the Second National Bank; E. B. Denison, a large land owner and extensively engaged in farming; George H. Van Etten, ex-Mayor, lumberman and real estate owner; Isaac Marston, lawyer and Attorney General of the State; B. E. Warren, Cashier First National Bank; N. B. Bradley, present member of Congress for the district including Bay City; S. G. M. Gates and W. L. Fay, prominent lumbermen; S. T. Holmes, recently member of Congress from New York and law partner of Senator Conkling; George Lord, City Comptroller; H. M. Bradley, lumberman; Luther Westover, a retired banker; H. C. Moore, extensively engaged in lumber business; John Drake, deputy United States Collector; H. J. H. Schutjes, Catholic priest; H. H. Hatch, lawyer; Thos. Cranage, jr., lumberman; Appleton Stevens, a prominent lumberman and present Mayor of the city; Thomas Carney, sen., for many years Director of the Poor; C. M. Averell, prominently connected with the introduction of the towing system of the river, and prominent real estate owner; Harry Griswold, who was among the first to commence the erection of brick buildings in the city; George Campbell, a heavy real estate dealer and lumberman; Charles Scheurmann, now associated with B. Witthauer, in lumbering, both these gentlemen being old residents and prominent business men; Richard Scheurmann, in the boot and shoe trade; Albert Miller (not Judge Albert Miller), lumberman and member of the Common Council; Luther Beckwith, a prominent lawyer; Henry S. Raymond, ex-postmaster, and T. C. Phillips, present incumbent of that office; George Lewis, banker; Andrew Walton, lumberman; J. H. Yawkey and William C. Yawkey; John L. Dolsen, lumberman; L. A. Barber, lumberman; J. D. Lewis, President Board of Education; Descum Culver, lumberman; A. J. Cooke, merchant, L. L. Culver, lumberman; Frank Crandell, merchant; H. Tupper, physician; Geo. H. Shearer, lumberman and inventor; A. H. Van Etten, manager Wooden Ware Works; George Young, merchant; W. H. Fennell, County Treasurer; H. M. Fitzhugh, president Wooden Pipe Works; A. Folsom, lumberman; E. M. Fowler, lumberman; A. McDonell, lawyer; S. M. Green, Circuit Judge; C. F. Gibson, merchant; H. A. Gustin, merchant; John Haynes, lawyer; D. C. Smalley, machinery manufacturer; J. W. McMath, Judge of Probate; W. H. Miller, merchant; Winsor Scofield, City Attorney; Græme M. Wilson, Prosecuting Attorney; T. F. Shepard, lawyer; W. H. Tousey, merchant; M. Watrous, lumberman; N. Whittemore, Justice of the Peace. We might mention many others whose names will be honored by their fellow-citizens, from having taken a prominent part in the early development of the city, or being the first to step from a beaten track and introduce new systems of trade or branches of business. To C. R. Hawley & Co. belongs the credit of opening the first store in the city for the *exclusive* sale of dry goods, a venture looked upon at the time as of doubtful prudence. Their present magnificent store in the Cranage block, surrounded by other stores in the same exclusive line is sufficient evidence of the wisdom of the venture.

Cooke & Langworthy (now Cooke & Co., Munger block) were among the first to realize the importance of Bay City as a business point, and their large L store in the Shearer block, was for many years the centre of attraction with the ladies, a favoritism which continues to draw the fair sex to their present large and complete establishment in the Munger block. And here we may say that the dry goods stores of F. A. Bancroft & Co., L. Ehrlich and A. & I. Grabowsky, and the clothing houses of F. H. Blackman & Co., Grow Bros., Edwards & Co. B. Meister and Schott & Co., the grocery houses of Gibson & Bartlett, L. H. & J. Stanton, Ellsworth & Parish, Meisel & Goeschel, Wetherell & Hage, Shepherd & Meston, H. H. Gustin, Campbell & Tyler, Woodard Bros. and Fitzpatrick & Co., cannot be excelled in point of stocks, enterprise and all that conduces to a well-regulated business. Among the wholesale grocers of note are Gustin & Merrill and Supe & Rademacher. The former have one of the completest and most extensive stores in the State, which was constructed especially to accommodate their large trade, and is supplied with hoisters and grain elevators. Supe & Rademacher have a grain elevator on the Flint & Pere Marquette railway track, near Third street.

WENONA.

Next to Bay City, the largest of the thriving places in this county is Wenona. It has a village organization, but in population and business it is clearly entitled to rank with many a pretentious "city." Wenona is admirably situated on the west bank of the Saginaw river, directly opposite Bay City, with which it is connected by a railroad and a general road bridge. The location is high and dry, and affords many fine sites for residences, the most prominent of these, perhaps, being on Au Sable street, which runs north from Midland street, along a beautifully wooded ridge parallel to the river. Here are already some dwellings worthy of note, as evidences of excellent taste in the production of handsome and comfortable homes, the residences of a cultured people.

In a business point of view, the most noticeable of Wenona's advantages is her long stretch of river front, affording the best facilities for shipping by lake. This front is already well improved in many places. Upon it are located the mammoth saw-mills of H. W. Sage & Co., and all the other appurtenances of a first-class lumber and salt manufacturing establishment. The Jackson, Lansing & Saginaw railroad has extensive slips just south of the Sage property, and still above these are the ship-yards of Capt. James Davidson and Capt. P. B. Hitchcock. Below Sage's is the shipyard of Ballentine & Co., the most complete establishment of the kind in the Valley. From these yards have been launched some of the finest specimens of naval architecture of which the lake marine can boast. Besides the above-named establishments, there is a plaster mill operated by Smith, Bullard & Co., and supplied from their plaster-beds at Alabaster, and the Litchfield estate's saw-mill.

Midland and Linn streets are the principal business streets of Wenona. They have a number of handsome brick blocks, prominent among which are the Sage block, and the Babo, Aplin, Campbell, Allard, Moots and Bank blocks. These are all well-constructed business buildings, and would ornament the principal street of any western city. Several of the best of these were completed in 1874, the village sharing in the prosperity which made Bay City an exception among the cities of the State during that and the preceding year.

In the way of educational facilities, Wenona is well-provided. Her central school building is a handsome three-story brick, costing about $20,0000, and capable of seating 500 pupils. There are several churches and more are soon to be built. St. Paul's Episcopal Society has a chapel and will sonn erect a church edifice upon a fine site, centrally located. There is a Baptift mission, and full organizations of the Methodist and Presbyterian denominations, withh comfortable and commodious church buildings. The Catholics also have a prosperous organization, and the German Lutherans have lately built a church.

Wenona is well supplied with hotels, both in number and quality. The traveler will find few houses more comfortably and neatly provided, and better administered, than the Rouech House, a three-story brick on Linn street, and the principal hotel of the village. It is a first-class house. The Irwin House is located on Midland street, at the crossing of the J., L. & S. railroad, and is a commodious and well-kept house, having a fine livery stable attached, and affording generally all things necessary for the transient guest. These are the most prominent of the hotels, though there are several others to make up the bountiful supply of Wenona in this line.

The project of a water supply, principally for protection from fire, wae agitated in the fall of 1874, and the prospect was that the village would have such a supply before long. Several plans were under consideration, either of which would answer the purpose. At present the fire department consists of an excellent Clapp & Jones steam fire engine, with an efficient company.

Wenona has a fine farming country back of her limits, and this is being rapidly developed. The prosperity of the village is therefore well assured. When it is known that in 1863 there were but two buildings in Wenona, the magnitude of her growth since that time will be apparent.

A NEW SALT BASIN.

Bountiful as the supply of brine for the manufacture of salt has been heretofore, it has lately appeared that we have been only tapping the upper portion of the deposits. The following article, which we copy from the *Lumberman's Gazette* (Bay City,) of Sept. 5, 1874, gives an account of the new discoveries in this line:

The most important discovery which has been made in the Saginaw Valley or its vicinity for at least a score of years, has just been made at a point known as Blackmer's, about 14 miles from East Saginaw. At this point a boring for a salt well has just been completed at a depth of 1,764½ feet, where a-good supply of brine has been found. It is well known that all borings for brine in the vicinity of the Saginaw river are successful, and the mere fact that fourteen miles away there is brine is not in itself of much significance. The real importance of the discovery lies in the now well ascertained fact that the Blackmer well brine comes from a deposit never before reached.

The depth of the salt wells along the river varies from about 700 feet to over 1,000 feet. None of the borings in this immediate vicinity, therefore, have ever touched so low a depth as the Blackmer well reaches. Ii was at first supposed that the rock in which the brine is found at Blackmer's was the well known Onondaga formation, but Dr. C. Romiger, State Geologist, and Dr. S. S. Garrigues, State Salt Inspector, who have just made a careful examination of the new boring, agree that the Onondaga rock must be hundreds if not thousands of feet below the bottom of the new well. In short, an entirely new salt supply has been found, hundreds of feet below the source from which the river wells draw their brine.

The brine at Blackmer's is found in a very porous sandstone. The gentlemen above named, from whom we get this information, have no doubt of a practically inexhaustible supply of brine from the newly-found rock. It has not yet been thoroughly tested, and its precise strength determined, but enough is known to warrant the assertion that we have below us, and supplementing our present fine brine supply, a reservior as yet untouched, the exhaustion of which is beyond all human power, and which could be relied upon for the support of a salt manufacture ten times the extent of ours, if all the existing wells were to go dry to-morrow. Whatever may have been the doubts on that point, the boring at Blackmer's has effectually set them ot rest. A few hundred feet below the bottom of our deepest wells is a new and inexhaustible supply.

One effect of the boring at Blackmer's, in the opinion of Dr. Romiger, is to demolish the theory that a bed of rock salt underlies the Valley. Dr. Romiger now thinks the existence of such a bed extremely problematical, but the question has lost its old interest, now that we have a new supply of brine beyond all chance of exhaustion. The salt interest is forfeited anew, and as it never was before, by this most fortunate discovery.

A Joke of the Early Day—The Biter Bitten—A Fish and Rat Story.—In the early history of every thriving seaport town the gathering together of congenial spirits, whose lack of legitimate occupation, while waiting for something to turn up, was promotive of a spirit of fine and practical joking, is an almost inevitable certainty. Bay City was no exception to the rule. With boundless faith in the sure coming of that day of growth and prosperity which Bay City has since attained to so goodly an extent, there were gathered in her limits the elements of good fellowship, which delighted in a practical joke, either in giving or receiving. Among those early pioneers were our fellow citizens of to-day, Julius B. Hart and George Lord. Both these gentlemen owned fisheries on the Bay Shore contiguous to each other, where in proper seasons of the year, they caught and shipped to Detroit and other points, the results of their endeavors, often realizing large amounts of money from successful seasons, and at other times enjoying (?) the discomforts of "fisherman's luck" generally. Both enjoyed, and each knew how to give and take a joke. One cold bright morning in the fall of 18—, the two met near the foot of Third street, and after passing the compliments of the morning turned to separate, when Hart exclaimed, "By the way, Lord, I'd nearly forgotten; I was down to the shore this morning and Joe (Lord's foreman at the fishery) told me to tell you that the fish were running like blazes, and he wanted you to send him down a lot of dressers (men to dress and pack fish), salt and barrels." "Thunder!" shouted Lord, "Is that so?" and away he sped to pick up all the adepts in dressing fish he could find, and in an hour his large boat was loaded with fish barrels, salt and men, and ready to start for the shore, with Lord along to enjoy the rich harvest in prospect awaiting him. Just as the boat was shoved away from the dock to start on her trip, Hart came hurriedly to the dock with "Hold on, Lord, I've just heard from the shore again; the fish have stopped running, and Joe don't wan't any thing more than he's got." Lord saw that he was sold, the boat was hauled to the dock and unloaded, and with vengeance in his eye Lord went home studying revenge. Weeks passed by and the joke was almost forgotten by all who had enjoyed a hearty laugh at Lord's expense. Not so with the chief victim, however. His opportunity came at last. The saloon in the basement of the Wolverton House was *the* fashionable resort of that day, and looking in at the door one afternoon Lord spied Hart at the table with some friends, playing an innocent game of "Penny Ante." While he looked, an Indian entered with a muskrat skin, a commodity in which Hart dealt, and which it is said at one time bore the same relation to "legal tender," as shingles have often done at a time of scarcity of money. "Ugh!" said Lo, "Jule Hart you buy um skin?" "Yes," was the response, "give you ten cents, throw him over in that corner, here's your money." The Indian took the money, threw down the skin and departed, at which Hart returned his attention to the game, which was becoming interesting. Lord picked up the skin and unnoticed left the saloon. It was but a few moments before a young boy entered the saloon and sold Hart a rat skin, throwing it into the corner as directed, and receiving his pay. The game went on, interrupted every few moments by a rat skin trade. Skins came in stretched on shingles, and on doubled twigs, and unstretched. Hart bought them all. At last the day was drawing to a close, and the game came to an end. Hart rose from the table remarking, "I've lost at the game, but I've bought a thundering pile of skins this afternoon," and he threw his gratified eye over toward the corner where his skins had been deposited. "Whew!" was his exclamation as but a single skin met his vision, "who in thunder has stole my skins!" Lord, at the instant edging toward the door, remarked, "It's been almost as good a day for rats, as that morning was for fish, Jule." Hart saw that he was sold; he had paid out about five dollars on one rat skin, and Lord was made disbursing officer, to see that the price of that skin was duly appropriated for the general good, in the manner common to those days.

How a Young Lawyer Commenced his Career—A Minister the Victim of a Practical Joke.—In early days when hotels were scarce, new comers to the State of Michigan were forced to ask favors of the older settlers, which in these days would be looked upon as the height of presumption. Andrew C. was a young lawyer residing in the then small village of Lapeer, having but recently taken to himself a wife and commenced housekeeping. There was no hotel in the place, and travelers oft times made use of A. C.'s barn, sometimes without so much as saying "by your leave." A. C. had decided to remove to Bay City, and was making preparations to do so, when his barn was appropriated by a new comer to the neighborhood, who put a load of hay into the loft, and drove a cow into the yard to eat the hay. The evening before he left for Bay City, A. C. was in "the store" of the village, and met the Rev. Mr. Smith, a Congregational minister (afterwards settled in East Saginaw), who had but recently taken charge of the little flock about Lapeer. As they conversed, Mr. Smith remarked, "I wish I could buy a good cow." "Do you want a cow?" said A. C. "I'm glad you mentioned it, for there's one up at my barn which I can't take away with me. You can have her if you will, and there's a load of hay in the barn to feed her with." Profuse were the thanks of the reverend gentleman at so munificent a bequest. "But," said A. C., "I must tell you about her. She is the most peculiar cow you ever saw. She must be milked before five o'clock in the morning or you can't get her to give down a drop of milk." "Well, I am an early riser," said the dominie, "I can milk her before five, as well as after." A. C. moved to Bay City, and the minister was careful to milk his cow "before five o'clock" each morning, and a noble mess of milk she gave, and with liberality was the hay fed to her. Things went well for several days, until while milking, one morning, the parson's ears were shocked with the profane expletives of a voice which called him a thief, a robber, and sundry other pet names which to a minister were simply horrifying. "I've caught you at last you hypocritical, thieving parson; preaching honesty to the people, and robbing your neighbors of their milk. I'll break your ——— head," etc, etc. Rising from his milking stool the parson faced the irate farmer, who for a time would give him no chance to put in a word edgewise. "But it's my cow," at last got in the parson, "A. C. made me a present of her, and of the hay in the barn, the night before he left." Explanations ensued, and as both realized the sell, both enjoyed a hearty laugh, and were good friends. Those who know our fellow townsman, A. C., persist in saying that he still enjoys a practical joke, and loves to play them off on his friends.

A Big Mouth.—Squa-conning creek, empties into the Saginaw river but a short distance above Bay City, and further than to say that at its mouth is a creek of considerable size, we give no further description of it. Harry C., brother of that old Pioneer, our respected fellow citizen Judge C., resided in early days at Saginaw City, and was noted as an inveterate wag and practical joker. Having returned from a visit to the Judge at Bay City, Harry met a traveling dentist, who in his peregrinations had stumbled into the Saginaws, and was operating upon the mouths of the scattered settlers. "Doctor," said Harry, "I've just come up from the mouth of the river, and Squire Conning wanted me to send you down to fix up his mouth. It's a thundering big mouth and has'nt got a tooth in it." Elated with the prospect of a good job, the dentist jumped into a canoe (the only means of transit between the two places) and paddled to Portsmouth (now Seventh Ward, Bay City). Reaching there after eighteen miles of paddling, he made diligent inquiry for "Squire Conning," and his disgust may be better imagined than described, when he found that he had passed the Squire's mouth, some miles up the river.

The School Sleigh Ride.—Harry C. was the most popular school teacher in the Saginaw Valley, and for many years "taught the young idea how to shoot straight," in the humble school house of Saginaw City. Finding his scholars disposed on one occasion to be unruly, he coaxed them to obedience by the promise of a sleigh ride, as soon as snow came. The promise was enough, the unruly youths knew that it would not be forgotten, nor yet neglected, for their teacher always kept his word whether it was to reward or to punish. Good order and diligence in study resulted, and all looked forward with impatience to the advent of winter. At last it came, a good snow storm made glad the hearts of the youth, and ere many days the announcement was made that the sleigh ride would take place on a certain afternoon. The long looked for hour came at last, the expectant and hilarious scholars were gathered at the school house, awaiting the coming of the teacher with the team. At last he came in sight, and such a team, and such a shout as the scholars raised, as Harry drove up to the school house door, with a diminutive donkey hitched to a pair of bob-sleds. They piled upon the boards, boys and girls together, and they had their ride, and if they did not make Goldsmith Maid's time of 2:16, the survivors of the present day assure us that at the rate of two miles in sixteen hours, it was the most laughable and enjoyable sleigh ride of their lives.

From Saginaw to "Masho's" House and How they Got There.—When the early denizens of the Valley started out on a duck hunt, or a trip down the river, or into the woods, the gun, with powder, ball and shot, were no more essential elements for success or comfort on the expedition than was the jug or bottle of whisky. This was of course in the times when everybody drank whisky and no evil was *thought*, whatever may have resulted from its use. Gardner Williams, "Lixa Boga" and Major Moseby, all long since departed this life, jumped into their canoe at Saginaw City one afternoon and paddled down the river to Masho's house, which was situated not far from McGraw's present mill. It was late when they started, and the shades of night came on long before they reached the head of Crow Island. Meantime sundry lunches had been taken from the jug in the bow of the canoe, and all was merry. At last the voyagers concluded that they must be almost down to Masho's, and began to scan the shore. The rice marshes near Willow Island were taken for those which led to Masho's, and carefully they pulled themselves through the long grass, wondering what had become of the eagerly sought for dwelling. All night they worked among the tall grass, until the gray light of the morning disclosed to them the fact that they were seven miles from Masho's, and that their sanguine hopes had been more the wonderful effect of their brown jug in dispelling distance, than a reality. It was breakfast time when the three wearied and dispirited men reached their destination, where the justice done to their breakfast, was good evidence that they had been disappointed in their supper of the night before.

A Bear Story—Shooting Ducks with a Bear Charge.—It is within the recollection of many present citizens of Bay City, and they by no means very ancient in point of years, when bears were roaming the woods within its present limits. An inveterate joker from the up river village, on occasion of a visit to his brother at Bay City (Lower Saginaw as it was then), stopped at the hostelry of our esteemed citizen, Judge Campbell, (who had recently built the hotel since known as the "Globe," on the corner of what is now Water and Fifth streets, although its original size bore little semblance to its present proportions.) As "joker" sat in an easy chair toasting his shins by the fire, his brother entered in a hurry with the declaration to "joker," "There's a big bear just out in the woods." Guns were always in readiness for sport, and it was but a few moments before the joker, led by his brother and one or two other friends, was hurrying through the stumps of the clearing which extended almost to Washington street. Cautiously feeling their way through the woods, they reached a point not far from the present site of the Court House, when joker was shown the bear, which proved to be a very large coal black hog belonging to the brother, his pilot. After a good laugh, the party wended its way back to the house. Joker watched his chance by the way, to separate from the rest, and to place in the gun a charge about six inches deep. On reaching the house the gun was carelessly placed in the corner, and the company about the fire indulged in a series of jokes and the enjoyment of a good time generally. Presently joker left the house and went down to the river bank, about in the rear of the present Jennison block, returning presently with the carelessly imparted information that there was "a thundering flock of ducks just settled in the river." "We'll have some for supper," exclaimed his brother, and seizing the gun from the corner, cautiously picked his way to a favorite log on the river bank, behind which he was accustomed to lay in wait for the feathered tribes. Joker and the rest of the company followed behind, and watched the sport. With the breech to his shoulder, and the barrel resting on the log, sportsman blazed away at the innocent ducks. It was hard to tell which end of the gun killed most. Sportsman fell back on the ground with his left hand to his right shoulder, in his agony, asking between paroxysms of pain, "What the thunder had got into that gun." "Why, you foolish fellow," said joker, "you've been trying to shoot ducks with a bear charge." All present saw the point of the joke, and it is said joined in attempting to relieve the sufferer, by copious applications of whisky internally and externally.

The Publisher's Miscellany.

There has been considerable delay in getting out this little book, but it has been owing to the inability of the publisher to give his undivided attention to the work. There have been obstacles in the way which it was impossible to foresee, and which have been overcome with no little difficulty. With scarcely an exception, the project of this work has been kindly encouraged by words and deeds on the part of the public, and because of the interest shown in the work on the part of those for whose benefit it was designed, the publisher has naturally felt the greater anxiety to accomplish a creditable result. The plan of the work has been enlarged and improved several times since it was first commenced.

As to the contents, it may be said that it has been more difficult to decide what could be omitted, than it has to find subject matter that deserved to go in. Many subjects were abbreviated much more than was desired, in order to bring the whole within limits prescribed. For this reason there are in some parts an incompleteness which will be noticed by the reader who is conversant with the subjects treated. Indeed it has not been so much the aim of the work to secure perfection as to prepare a compilation of facts concerning the early history, commercial advantages and future prospects of Bay City that will serve every resident as a valuable book of reference for some years to come, and especially that shall attract strangers, men of business, enterprise and capital, to seek here for successes that bid fair to be easily attainable. In other words, we urge that this is a work which *every one who is interested in the growth and prosperity of Bay City should place in the hands of one or more of his friends or acquaintances with a view to inducing them to take up a residence here, and engage in some one of the various branches of industry that promise so well for the future.*

The price of this publication is not so high but that every one with a home here, can and should have a copy for their own use, while many are able to procure several copies for judicious distribution abroad. The numerous illustrations which embellish the work, render it attractive and quite appropriate as a present from one friend to another.

If the efforts of the publisher have resulted in pleasing the public for whom the service has been performed, such appreciation will be a reward gratefully acknowledged.

C. C. WHITNEY,

Druggist and Pharmacist,

City Drug Store

A large and complete stock of

Drugs and Patent Medicines,

Constantly kept on haud,

AT LOW PRICES.

Wholesale Agent for the celebrated

Compound Syrup of Tar

FOR COUGHS AND COLDS.

ED. WOOD & CO.,

THE

JEWELERS.

A LARGE STOCK OF

FINE WATCHES,

Clocks and Jewelry,

Silver and Plated Ware.

☞ A full stock of goods always on hand.

Watson Block, 101 North Water St.

ED. WOOD. JAS. A. WELLS.

JACKSON, LANSING AND SAGINAW RAILROAD LANDS.

VALUABLE

PINE AND FARMING LANDS

FOR SALE.

The attention of lumbermen and capitalists desiring profitable investments is called to the land grant lands of the JACKSON, LANSING & SAGINAW RAILROAD COMPANY, now offered for sale at low prices and upon easy terms. The grant was made at an early day, before the pine timbered lands had been entered, and embraces some of the choicest lands to be found in Michigan. The railroad is constructed and in operation from Jackson to Town Range 3 west, a distance of 235 miles, and will soon be completed to the Straits of Mackinaw. Particular attention is called to the large tracts of the best

WHITE AND NORWAY PINE TIMBER

Along the line of the road, and upon the Au Sable, Cheboygan, Muskegon and Manistee Rivers, which are now the most important logging streams in this State. It is confidently believed that this Company offers greater inducements to purchasers of pine lands than can be found elsewhere. The farming lands of the Company include some of the most fertile and well watered hardwood lands in the State. Especial attention is called to the farming lands in Crawford, Otsego and Cheboygan Counties, which are high and rolling, timbered mainly with the finest hard maple, soil black sandy loam, and abounding in springs of the purest water. These counties are being rapidly settled, and the lumbering business in the vicinity will afford to farmers a first-rate market for produce for many years.

TERMS OF SALE.

For pine lands, one-fourth down and the remainder in three equal annual installments, with interest at seven per cent.—must be paid before the timber can be cut. For farming lands to settle, longer time will be given if desired.

For lists of lands, further information, or purchase, apply to

O. M. BARNES,

Land Commissioner,

LANSING, MICH.

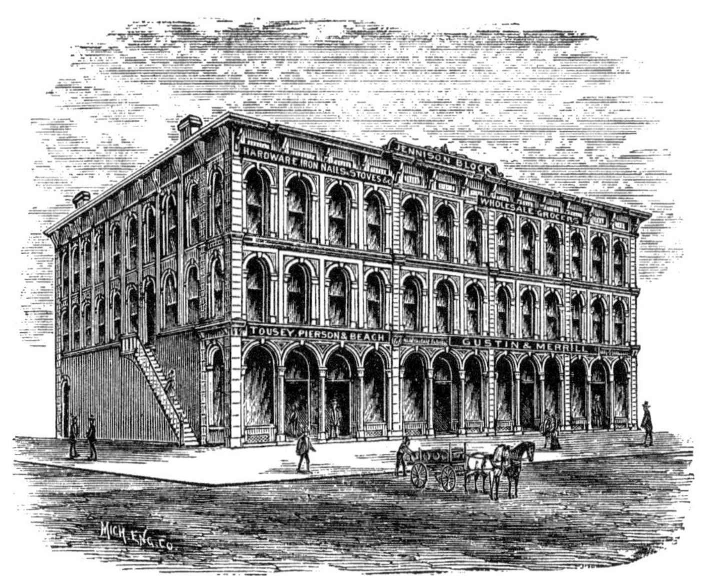

Tousey, Pierson & Beach,

Dealers in

HARDWARE.

Manufacturers Agents for

Henry Disston & Son's Saws,

AT FACTORY PRICES.

American File Co.'s and Jowett's English Files.

Fairbrother's Belting,

BUILDERS',

Mill and Lumbermen's Supplies.

Sole Agents in Bay City for

Detroit Stove Works' Stoves.

Jennison Block, Water St.,

BAY CITY, MICH.

R. P. GUSTIN. H. P. MERRILL.

GUSTIN & MERRILL,

WHOLESALE GROCERS

And Commission Merchants.

JOBBERS IN

Flour, Feed, Oats, Hay

And Lumbermen's Supplies.

☞ Feed mill in connection with Elevator in Jennison Block, Bay City.

Hay, Oats and Produce shipped direct from Elevator at Mt. Morris to customers along lines of Railway.

They are prepared to receive consignments by water to their new Iron Warehouse on the Dock.

Goods shipped to customers up Shore, dockage free.

Jennison Block Bay City, Mich.

THE BAY CITY TRIBUNE.

Daily and Weekly.

The Leading Newspaper of Northern Michigan.

TERMS OF THE DAILY TRIBUNE:

Delivered by Carrier, per month in advance . $ .65	By mail, per annum in advance $6.00
Delivered by Carrier, per quarter in advance . 1.80	By mail, per month in advance 50

TERMS OF THE WEEKLY TRIBUNE:

By mail, per annum in advance $1.50	By mail, four months in advance . . . . . $ .50

Advertising Rates Liberal. Circulation Largest in the Valley.

Address, TRIBUNE CO., Bay City, Mich.

RICHARD SCHEURMANN,

Wholesale and Retail Dealer in

Boots and Shoes,

WATSON BLOCK,

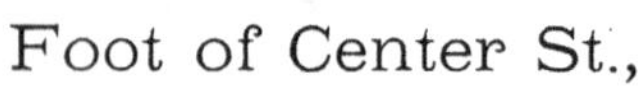

Foot of Center St., BAY CITY, MICH.

ALONZO CHESBROUGH, PRESIDENT. J. P. PHILLIPS, VICE-PRESIDENT. ORRIN BUMP, CASHIER.

The State Bank of Bay City.

Capital and Surplus, $160,000.

BOARD OF DIRECTORS. — Alonzo Chesbrough, Chas. G. Southworth, J. P. Phillips, Hon. S. T. Holmes, Hon. L. Westover, Andrew Walton, Orrin Bump.

☞ Gold, Canada Funds and Foreign Exchanges bought and sold. Collections made and returns promptly remitted.

THE SECOND NATIONAL BANK

OF BAY CITY.

Capital, - - $100,000.

WM. WESTOVER, President. *JOHN McGRAW, Vice-President*

W. L. PLUM, Cashier.

BOARD OF DIRECTORS. —Wm. Westover, John McGraw, H. W. Sage, A. J. Cooke, W. H. Tousey, Hon. Albert Miller, D. C. Smalley, Alex. McFarlan, Wm. B. McCreery, Wm. L. Smith, W. L. Plum.

☞ Gold, Canada Funds and Foreign Exchanges bought and sold. Collections made and returns promptly remitted.

Shearer's Patent Log Turner

Patented Feb. 3, 1874

By G. H. Shearer of Bay City.

FOR SAW MILLS.

I HAVE ALSO FOR SALE

Gang Lath Mills.

For further information apply to or correspond with

GEO. H. SHEARER, Bay City, Michigan.

The only Republican Morning Daily in Michigan, North of Detroit.

DAILY AND WEEKLY

CHRONICLE

TERMS:

DAILY—Fifteen cents per week, delivered.
$7.00 per annum, by mail.

WEEKLY—(Quarto) $2.00 per annum, in advance.

Published by the CHRONICLE ASS'N,
Chronicle Building, Water St., Bay City, Mich.

Book and Job Printing Department the Largest in Northern Michigan.

JAS. SHEARER & CO.,

Manufacturers and Dealers in

Lumber, Lath, Etc.

Cor. Water and First Sts.,

BAY CITY, MICH.

Bay City Transit Railway.

Among the more important of the enterprises which have promoted the growth and advancement of Bay City, may be named the "Bay City and Portsmouth" Street Railway now known as the "Bay City Street and Transit Railway," chartered by the Common Council in 1865. The company originally built its track from Third street, Bay City, to a point now known as Thirty-fifth street, formerly Portsmouth, now the Seventh Ward. This road following the river line on Water street, passing all the mills and manufactories, has added not a little to the development of the city. During the past year the franchise has passed into the hands of a company of capitalists who are largely interested in the different enterprises centering in Bay City, who have extended the line of track to the north about two miles, to the mills nearest the mouth of the river, and south to a connection with the track of the F. & P. M. R. W., at McGraw's mill, crossing the track of the D. & B. C. and J., L. & S. R. R. near the railroad bridge, which is near to the center of business in the city. The new company, with an increased capital, have laid a light T rail of sufficient strength to enable them to do the work of a transit road, and during the winter of 1874–5 will commence to deliver empty and loaded cars, at, and from any mill between the mouth of the river and McGraw's mill (a distance of six miles), to any of the railroads now or hereafter centering in the city, thus affording mill owners on the river all the facilities for winter and inland trade enjoyed by mills located on the lines of railroads. The road will be operated by dummy engines, which will transfer railroad cars by night, the track being operated by horses through the day.

The effect of this arrangment will readily be seen, in advantages which can be boasted by no other city in the West, not to say the nation, bringing as it does, a river frontage of six miles, with twenty-nine saw and shingle mills and twenty salt manufactories, and unlimited room for additions to the number, in direct connection with railroads leading to all parts of the nation, while not interfering with the daily use of the road for local street passage traffic. It is the intention of the company to extend the track to Wenona whenever that place shall become an integral portion of the city, so as to come under the operation of the company's charter. The officers of the company are as follows:

President, James Clements.
Treasurer, Phillip Bach.
Secretary, James D. Warner.

MASON & McNEIL,

Munger Block, Center St.

A Full Line of all Goods Usually Found in a First Class Drug Store.

SPECIAL ATTENTION

Paid to Prescription Department.

GEO. LEWIS, Pres't. GEO. H. YOUNG, Cash'r

Bay City Bank

Cor. Center and Saginaw Sts.,

BAY CITY, MICH.

Cash Capital, $100,000.

DIRECTORS:

William Peter, Geo. W. Budington, Geo. Young, George H. Young, George Lewis.

Drafts Sold for all Parts of the United States and Europe.

☞ Interest paid on deposits in savings department.

NORTHWESTERN

GAS AND WATER PIPE CO.

Main Office and Works, Bay City, Mich.

CHICAGO OFFICE, 144 DEARBORN STREET.

THE NORTHWESTERN GAS AND WATER PIPE COMPANY, incorporated under the provisions of the mining and manufacturing laws of Michigan, commenced business about the 1st of June, 1871. Since that time it has manufactured more than a million feet of various sizes of gas and water pipe, which have been sent into the States of West Virginia, Ohio, Indiana, Michigan, Illinois, Wisconsin, Minnesota, Iowa, Missouri, Kansas, Nebraska, Tennessee, Mississippi, Louisiana and Nevada, also the Territories of Colorado and Utah, and the Dominion of Canada. Wherever used it has given entire satisfaction, aud the increased demand requiring large additions to the manufacturing facilities of the company, is the best proof that the Wyckoff Gas and Water Pipe possesses all the excellence claimed for it, and all the qualities required for perfect water and gas mains.

The pipe is made of white pine logs bored out with the Wyckoff patent core augur, of any required size, in sections eight feet long. The logs are turned off in a lathe to remove the sap, and the ends are chambered out to receive the thimbles or connections. Each section of water pipe is then banded spirally with the best band iron of such weight as may be required by the pressure to which it is to be subjected in use, and afterwards is carefully and thickly coated with asphaltum or coal tar pitch, to protect the iron bands from rust, and the exterior of the wooden shell from the atmosphere.

We claim that the Wyckoff Pipe thus constructed, presents the most perfect combination yet discovered of durability, strength, purity and cheapness, and is the best water main in use for cities, villages, farms, country seats, railroads, mines, distilleries, tanneries, breweries, etc., etc. The ease and rapidity with which this pipe can be laid in the trenches, and the great facility with which it may be tapped for the purpose of forming connections are circumstances greatly in its favor.

The Wyckoff Water Pipe of our manufacture, is laid down in connection with the Holly system of water works in Bay City and Saginaw City, Mich., also with the Dean Bros' pumps at Union City, Indiana; under reservoir head at Bellaire, Crestline and New Lisbon, Ohio, and Grand Rapids, Mich., with stand pipe service South Bend, Indiana, and also to some extent in the city of Chicago. It has also been furnished to the following railroads in large quantities, viz: The Michigan Central; Jackson, Lansing and Saginaw; Canada Southern; Ohio and Mississippi; Union Pacific; Northern Pacific; Chicago, Burlington and Quincy; Alton and St. Louis; Lake Shore and Michigan Southern, and others.

The following gas companies have our gas pipe in use, viz: Saginaw City, Flint, Hillsdale, Mich; River Side and Hyde Park, Ill.; Lawrence, Atchison and Topeka, Kansas; Janesville, Ripon, Kenosha and Racine, Wis.; Lancaster, Mansfield, Alliance, and many other places in Ohio, Tennessee and Mississippi.

We respectfully refer all those who contemplate putting in gas or water works, or making extensions to those already in operation, to any of the above consumers of our pipe. We also invite correspondence with our home or Chicago office, where prompt attention will be given to all communications.

www.ingramcontent.com/pod-product-compliance
Lightning Source LLC
LaVergne TN
LVHW021424110826
845150LV00007B/2069

* 9 7 8 1 4 2 5 5 0 8 4 4 9 *